Complete Guide to Selling Your Business

Maximize Business Value and Increase Personal Wealth

Kelly Shaw

Trevin Rasmussen

Complete Guide to Selling Your Business
Copyright © 2009 by Kelly Shaw, Trevin Rasmussen

Published by Business Brokerage Services, LLC
P.O. Box 1369
Eagle, ID 83616
ISBN (978-0-692-00385-5)

Printed in USA

Acknowledgement

The authors would like to thank all their clients, friends, and family who have shared their time, talents, and wisdom over the years. It has been a privilege to associate with so many professionals who have, each in their own way, added to the success and knowledge of the authors. Being able to do their job with so many wonderful people has been a joy.

Table of Contents

Introduction

Did you know that only 20% of all the businesses on the market will be sold? Even more surprising is that only 2% of the people looking to buy a business will successfully complete the process. These are amazing facts that may cause you to ask why is it so hard to successfully transfer business ownership? The intent of this book is to help you understand the selling process so you can be prepared to successfully transfer business ownership.

This book explores the factors that all business owners must consider before selling their business. We will describe the most important steps for preparing your business for sale. We will also outline the process of selling your business and highlight the key elements for maximizing business value and increasing personal wealth. All through this book we will share real life examples to illustrate the principles discussed and point out the mistakes that others have made along the way with the intent to help you avoid the pitfalls on the road to selling your business.

It is important to remember that every business, seller, and buyer is different with varying needs, desires, and goals. This combination makes it impossible to predict the exact sale cycle of any business. However, there are some guidelines, systems, and standards that can be applied to any transaction. This guide is meant to inform the seller on what to expect, what is required, and what should be considered in the process of selling your business. Without question the most important part of this book is the step-by-step process that is provided. It will help you understand the process, timing, and sequence of events.

As we considered the purpose of the book we felt that not only did we want to explain the process of selling, but we also wanted to show business owners how they can "maximize business value and increase personal wealth." Most businesses owners have a real commitment and connection to their business. They want the business to continue, their employees to be protected, and they want to maximize the value of the business in the sale and create real wealth after the sale of the business. This book will show you how.

Who should read this book?

Every business owner will eventually exit his or her company and turn the reigns over to somebody else. How you handle the transition is the difficult part. You should be reading this book so you are informed about the process, the people involved, and the ways for increasing personal wealth and maximizing business value. Anyone who owns a business that wishes to create wealth by selling his or her business should read this book

Each year almost one million privately held small and mid-sized businesses are sold. These include retail shops, restaurants, service companies, manufacturing operations, and agriculture businesses – just to name a few. The owners of these companies are hard working people that achieved success by creating, providing, or distributing a product or service that is valuable. They have knowledge and expertise in a particular industry, know how to manage people and money, and are striving to provide a quality standard of living for their families and employees. If you are reading this book, it is likely that we are describing you!

The process of selling your business can be very exciting time for the business owner who has worked hard building something of value. It all starts with a decision that is very difficult to make and even more difficult to complete. The intent of this book is to take the mystery out of the process and to help you prepare for the future. We hope this book will help you understand the process for MAXIMIZING BUSINESS VALUE AND INCREASING PERSONAL WEALTH.

Now that we have laid the groundwork, lets' get started.

Chapter 1 – Deciding to Sell Your Business

Let's face it; you have to exit your business sometime. How you do this depends on a host of factors that need to be carefully considered. The decision to sell your business is more of a process with years of planning then an instantaneous, gut feel, or knee-jerk reaction. The odds of successfully transferring business ownership are significantly increased if the selling process begins several years prior to listing the business for sale or taking the business to the market. Unfortunately, most business owners haven't invested enough time or resources preparing the business to be sold. Not to worry, your business can still be successfully sold.

Should I sell my business now or later? Will my business be worth what I think it is worth? Should I sell to a competitor, individual, partnership, or a loyal employee? Will I have enough money to fund the next phase of my life? Can I sell my business by myself or do I need a business broker? These are all questions you have probably asked yourself at one time or another. They are probably the same questions that caused you to read this book. The answers to these questions will become part of the total equation for deciding to sell your business.

Some other the factors that cause a business owner to sell their business include retirement, death, divorce, competition, finances, or poor health – just to name a few. If you have the choice to sell your business on your own terms and conditions at a time in your life that makes sense, then you should feel very fortunate. We see poor economic conditions and competitive markets forcing business owners to sell at the absolute worst time. Keep in mind that the goal of any business owner should be to maximize business value while increasing personal worth.

Making your business sellable

The first step in the decision making process is determining if your business is sellable. The reality is that not all businesses are. And many business owners are in denial about this fact. It is hard to admit that your largest investment – being the business you own – isn't worth being sold. Remember that only 1 in 5 businesses on the market will be successfully sold. Pause for a minute and consider why the other 4 businesses didn't sell. Below is a list of possible reasons why businesses don't sell.

- The business is overpriced
- Poor financial performance
- Seller requires too much cash upfront
- Poor financial records
- Too much debt or leverage
- Too many minority partners
- Poor location
- Market position is weak
- Lack of quality employees
- Poorly packaged and presented
- Seller isn't sincerely motivated to sell
- Legal problems

The list could go on and on. But to make things simple there are really on two reasons why a businesses don't sell. First, the business is overpriced. This has as much to do with the owner's unrealistic expectations as it does with business valuation methodologies. Too many small business owners are hearing stories of companies that sell for ridiculous multiples. The result is a feeling that their business is worth way more then it actually is.

Second, the owner of the business is not sufficiently motivated to sell. They don't have a plan for what comes next. And they don't a have a way to fund that next phase of their life even if they did. These factors take away from the seller's motivation. If we were to examine businesses that have sold, you will find the reverse is true.

Now we are not trying to say that every sold business is free of the issues listed above. Rarely is a business without problems when it sells. In fact all businesses have issues that make the sale process difficult at best. And we are not suggesting that all issues have to be resolved before proceeding. Part of the process of deciding to sell your business is to determine if you have addressed the four most important elements in selling a business.

1. Asking Price
2. Terms and Conditions
3. Presentation of the Business
4. Attracting Qualified Buyers

You should consider how each of these factors would affect your success in selling your business.

Asking Price

The *asking* price and the *selling* price are two completely different things. Based on the historical data of thousands of closed transactions, businesses will sell for 80% of the asking price. That means either asking price is too high, or buyers are better negotiators than sellers. Having worked in the industry for many years we know that buyers are not necessarily better negotiators than seller. The problem is unrealistic expectations with the asking price.

Sellers are notorious for having unrealistic expectations about the value of their business. In almost in every case a seller will value the business more than the buyer will value the business. The seller has generally spent the better part of their life working the business. They know the success, and ultimate survival, of the business came with a heavy price. This history and attachment to the past causes the seller to generally over-value the business. Buyers on the other hand are dreaming unrealistically of becoming the next Warren Buffet and are looking for businesses that will improve dramatically with the infusion of the buyer's genius. Buyers buy businesses because they expect to do at least as good as the current seller if not better. Unfortunately, buyers don't have that love attachment to the company and they want to value the company at a rock bottom price.

Sellers measure a successful transaction by the selling price. Buyers measure a successful transaction by the discount they received off the asking price. The magical meeting of the minds occurs when both parties have accomplished their goal.

Having a business broker provide a Brokers Opinion of Value (BOV) or a licensed business appraiser prepare a Certified Valuation Analysis (CVA) will help bridge the gap between the buyer and seller. There may be good reasons for the asking price to be initially a little higher then the actually acceptable selling price. Creating a little room for negotiations may be a good strategy. You have to be careful about inflating the asking price too much so that you don't deter would-be-buyers based on the business being overpriced. Remember, everything is for sale at the right price. Getting the right price is critical in determining if now is the right time to sell.

Terms and Conditions

The next critical factor is the terms and conditions. Only 5% of all transactions are full cash purchases. And generally it is for businesses worth less than $100K in value. Almost always a seller is required to finance a portion of the sale with seller financing or a carry-back of a portion of the sale price.

Flexible terms and conditions will lead to a more sellable business at a higher price. The general rule of thumb is the higher the cash down payment the lower the total over-all price. The lower the cash down payment and the higher the seller financing the higher the total over-all price. It goes without saying that the seller needs to evaluate the risk of financing the buyer and collecting the debt. The seller needs to ensure that the buyer has something to loose so it is more difficult for them to walk away from the deal. Finding the right terms and conditions can be a real balancing act. Terms and conditions may be a factor in your determination to sell the business.

Marketing the Business for Sale

How the business is marketed for sale is generally a major factor in determining when and how to sell the business. Sellers generally want complete confidentiality in the process. This is also one of the major reasons to involve a professional business broker to manage the selling process.

Marketing the business for sale takes time and effort, know-how, and expertise to do it right. How the facts of the business are presented along with the biographical story will connect the buyer to the process and cause them to become emotionally invested. People want to feel like they are buying something special. That can only happen if the business is presented in such a way that it is informative, believable, and professional. Successfully completing this task generally requires some expert help.

We know of a man who wanted to sell his company by himself. So rather than hire a business broker he tried to put a few things together for potential buyers. He thought it would be a good idea to prepare a packet of information with a financial statement, a brief write-up about the company, and a business card so potential buyers could contact him. He sent the information to a handful people that he thought would be interested in buying his business. A few days went by and nobody called. Then a call came in from a competitor who just wanted to know why the business owner was selling – he had no desire to purchase the company. Pretty soon rumors began to circulate that the company was struggling to stay in business. The employees confronted the business owner with their concerns. In the end, the business owner spent a significant amount of time answering questions about the welfare of his business and resolving concerns. He lost some customers, a valuable employee, and learned a very important lesson about marketing a business. After this experience he called us and we began the process of selling his business professionally, confidentially, and successfully.

Attracting Qualified Buyers

The final factor in determining if you have a sellable business is whether or not it will attract qualified buyers. Basic math suggests that the more people who see your business for sale the better the chance you have of finding the right buyer. But exposing you business to hundreds of potential buyers comes with a risk. Many business owners are very nervous, and rightfully so, about the need for confidentiality. Unscrupulous people may use confidential or proprietary information about your business and do you harm. Maintaining confidentiality throughout the selling process is absolutely essential.

The trick is to generate maximum exposure to potential buyers while protecting the confidentiality of the seller's business. In order to maintain confidentiality, exposure to potential buyers must be handled by an intermediary such as a business broker. They know how to get the needed exposure and still protect the confidentiality of the transaction by providing a shield between the seller and the buyer.

Attracting buyers is only part of the job. You must be able to qualify the buyer as well. A qualified buyer is one that has the financial capacity to purchase the business and the necessary business expertise to be successful. Most business transactions involve some form of commercial financing. The requirements for obtaining a loan from a lender are becoming increasingly strict. All lenders will look at three things: (1) Strength of the business, (2) Strength of the buyer, and (3) the collateral to secure the loan.

A business broker can qualify buyers early in the process and save a lot of wasted time when the buyer goes to a lender and cannot get approved for a loan. A ready, willing, and "unable" buyer causes frustration for everyone involved in the process of selling a business. Let the business broker weed out the unable – or unqualified – buyers long before an offer is made.

Remember that the intent in selling is to create wealth and let the company continue to prosper. Therefore, the more you realize the value of these four important factors the greater chance you have at creating wealth with the sale of your business. Each of these factors plays a crucial role in determining to sell your business.

Knowing the right time to sell your business

When is the best time to sell your business? The majority of business owners get this question wrong. If you asked most business brokers they would tell you that about 90% of the businesses they sell are on the market at the wrong time. Only about 10% of the business have done their homework and are selling at the right time. This is less about timing the market and more about preparing for the sale. Certainly there is some timing involved, however; the majority of the problems are internal factors a business owner controls.

Let's consider the reasons to sell that you can NOT control.

- Divorce.
- Death in the family
- Loss of key employee
- Health issues
- Market conditions that force a sale
- Excessive debt
- Death of a partner

17

These issues often force the sale of a business at the wrong time. When a business is forced to sell at the wrong time, the owners of the business will not get maximum dollar for the business or generate as much personal wealth.

The owner that prepares for the eventual sale of their business will generate the greatest benefits. So when is the right time to sell? Generally speaking the best time to sell a business is when many of the following are in your favor:

- Sales and profits have consistently increased for 3 years
- You are outperforming your competition and increasing market share
- You have exclusive rights, territories, or customers
- Your customer list is growing
- You have little or no bad debt
- You have well documented processes, systems, and policies
- You have managers in place that can run the business without you involved
- You are in a personal position to offer flexible terms and conditions on the sale
- You can stay on long enough to transfer your knowledge and skill to the new owner
- You don't have minority partners that might complicate the sale

Those are just a few of the factors to be considered when selling a business. Later in the book we will discuss some other things you can do to maximize the value of your business. The list is very valuable and will give some insight on how to maximize the sales price. If you can accomplish the majority of items on the list you will have prepared your business for a successful sale.

Understanding market conditions

It is true that the market can affect the price and success of your business selling. Even in the worst of times the best of businesses will successfully sell and for a premium price. The question to ask yourself is this, "will holding my business until the market improves create more wealth for me now or in the future?"

Let's say that you have a choice to invest the proceeds of the sale now with a 6% return annually; or, you can continue owning your company and increase the profits at 10% annually. You will be better off owning your company and selling it later.

Most business brokers will tell you that market timing is less important than preparation. That is why successful business owners learn to work *on* their businesses rather than *in* their businesses. This means that if you spend time working on improving your business by establishing processes, systems, markets, and products you will increase your chances of successfully selling your business. If you spend all day working in your business trying to just get everything done as if it were a job, you won't increase the value of your business and potential buyers will recognize the risk of the business failing when you walk away. Quality businesses sell for higher prices no matter what the market is doing.

Factors to consider when selling a business

There are many personal and business factors to consider when selling a business. We will list a few of them here and give a brief explanation of what to consider in the process.

Does the sale need to be confidential?

You certainly will have a better chance at finding the right buyer if the sale is not confidential. However, most sales are done confidentially to protect the business from unintended consequences. Even with the best intentions to maintain the fact that the business is for sale, sometimes the word gets out. If it does leak out, you need to know how to you handle your employees, customers, and competition. That is why it is sometimes better to just handle that right up front rather than trying to put out the fire later. How you handle confidentiality is something to consider and discuss with your business broker. A professional business broker can help you understand how and what systems are used to insure the confidential nature of the sale.

Do I need a business broker or intermediary?

We discuss this at length in a later section of this book. As business brokers we believe the service we provide is valuable, otherwise we wouldn't do it. There is a long list of benefits that a business broker provides. However, we often come across situations where the owner of the business is quite capable of selling the business without the services of a business broker.

The types of businesses that don't need the help of a business broker are usually very small or very large companies. A very small company is one worth less than $100,000, has a handful of employees, and the role of the owner is more of a job than an owner. A very large company is one worth tens of millions of dollars. These companies are usually very well known and the targets of industry consolidations or candidates for going public with an IPO (Initial Public Offering).

How do I find a buyer?

The Internet is quickly becoming the number one source for buyer referrals. Print media and direct mail are the other primary mediums for finding potential buyers. The Internet has created an environment where buyers can research and analyze business opportunities without every speaking to the business owner or business broker. This is somewhat unfortunate for both buyers and sellers. Buyers are relying too much upon the limited financial and biographical information shared and do not come to appreciate the complete story of the business.

Perhaps the easiest way to find a buyer is to tap into the database of buyers already registered with a business broker. They have literally hundreds of individuals, groups, and companies that come to them looking for business opportunities. The good business brokers will track buyer information and have a method for identifying potential buyers for your business.

Do I have to carry or finance a portion of the sale?

The simple answer to this is yes. Only 5% of all business sales are cash sales and most of those are for businesses that sell for less than $100K. It is in the buyers' best interest to keep the seller connected to the company and working for its success. Generally speaking you should anticipate financing a portion of the sales price. Remember, it's not always a bad thing to be the bank. You should earn interest on the money borrowed by the buyer and have some recourse on the assets of the business if things don't go well.

How long will it take?

It is very difficult to gauge how long it will take a business to sell. The best answer is approximately 9 to 12 months. Some will sell in 30 days, others in two years. One thing is for sure, if the business is priced right and the seller is motivated and prepared to offer flexible terms and conditions, then the odds of finding a suitable buyer will increase and the business will sell sooner.

Will I need an attorney and CPA?

Again the simple answer is yes. You could try to do it all by yourself but you will probably end up loosing more money in the long run by not seeking the advice of experts. Your business broker can help you with selecting the most qualified transaction attorneys and CPA if you don't currently have a relationship with one that is qualified.

What will the process cost?

For businesses worth less than $1,000,000 a business broker is going to generally charge a commission of 10% to 12% of the selling price for their services. For businesses worth more than $1,000,000 there is a vast variety of pricing but generally you will pay 10% up to about $3,000,000 in sale price and anything over that price will have a declining scale. The commission is based on the selling price and paid to the broker at the time of closing.

Experience has shown that you will get more buyers offering you a higher price by enlisting the services of a business broker. The exception to this rule is for small businesses that have a valuation of less than $250K, and especially those with valuations of less than $100K. It is possible to sell smaller businesses without using a business broker and paying their commission.

There will also be a cost for the advice of your accountant the work of your attorney. Closing cost for an escrow agent may be as little as a couple hundred dollars up to a couple thousand. Closing costs are typically shared between the buyer and the seller.

What will my tax consequences be?

Understanding the tax liabilities for transferring business ownership is a difficult task without the help of a professional that understands tax laws. Your tax liability can be a huge factor in selling your business. If you have to claim all of the proceeds of the sale as ordinary income, your tax liability may be as high as 39% in some cases and even more in others. If you can claim a capital gain on the sale it may be as low at 15%, or less, given the many tax law changes. Consider in advance how to position the sale to prepare for the tax consequences.

What will I do after the sale?

Most business owners don't think about what they will do after the sale. They just figure now is the time to do something different. However, unless you have a concrete plan of what comes next, your motivation to sell will not be sufficient to successfully transfer business ownership. Please take time and give it some thought. Retirement is a wonderful reason to sell your business. But what will you spend your time doing and will you have enough money to sustain your life style. If your reason isn't retirement and you are just moving on to the next phase of your life with new exciting challenges, what is that challenge and how do you plan to fund that next big venture?

What will I do with the money?

The goal of selling your business is to create wealth by converting equity into liquidity. The amount of money going into your pocket when the transaction is complete should be the aim of every deal. Don't be too focused on the price, rather, focus on the net proceeds you will have at closing and the total net proceeds after you have collected your seller carry-back and financing. There may be other terms – such as rent for property owned – that will add to the total net proceeds.

Another advisor that you may want to add to your team of experts is a financial advisor – somebody that can invest the money wisely or counsel you in ways that will preserve the wealth over time. A financial advisor has access to all kinds of financial tools. If the amount of money you have is significant, then you should take some extra time and precaution to find an advisor that has the knowledge and experience to handle large amounts of money.

Remember you are trying to maximize the value of your business to increase your personal wealth. Increasing your personal wealth is nothing if you cannot protect and preserve that wealth for you and your loved ones.

Chapter 2 – Preparing Your Business to Sell

We have already discussed the importance of preparing your business for sale several years prior to selling. What follows in this chapter are several ways to begin that preparation.

Making your business attractive to buyers

If you talk to anyone who has been around the industry for a long time they will all tell you the same things – Sizzle Sells. What do we mean by "sizzle?" Sizzle is that intangible difference that makes a business unique and special, different from the others on the market. It could even be a franchise that for every practical purpose is identical to all other franchises but the one with sizzle will sell. There are a number of factors to give your business sizzle.

Have a good story to tell

Buyers like to hear how the business started, the challenges you overcame, and the sacrifices you made that got the business where it is today. They don't want to buy just another business. They want to buy a business that is special, unique, and somehow different than everyone else. They want to feel like they are part of something that overcame the odds and achieved success. They want to live the "American Dream."

One of our past clients, we will call him Bill, was great at telling the story of how his fertilizer manufacturing company was started. He described the process of clearing away sagebrush for new farmland and how the first couple of years the crops did absolutely great. But after a couple of years the weeds moved in and the bugs started eating the crops and the farmers began to struggle. The farmers couldn't understand what had changed. At this point in story Bill created a need for his unique blend of biological and conventional fertilizers that replace the natural bacteria and microorganisms that existed in years one and two of growing. He then goes on to give several examples of how his product helped the farmers to increase the yield and quality of the crops.

Throughout his story he is relating anecdotal evidence of his companies success. Bill talks about his interactions with JR Simplot (one of the worlds largest suppliers of fertilizer), his position on the state agriculture committee, and his relationship with the state universities. He shares this information modestly without bragging or sounding to good to be true.

Now lets analyze the story telling of another past client – we will call him Fred. He owned and operated one of the world's most popular franchises. Fred started with one store and expanded to six. When he would tell the story of how his company began, he couldn't resist the temptation of criticizing the franchise, its operations, and the decisions of the franchise leaders. He would dwell too much on the employee challenges and the headaches they caused him.

Fred's anecdotal stories included how the toilet would get plugged and how the cooler would break down. Most buyers at this point were looking for the exit. To make matters worse, Fred would get overly emotional when talking about his reasons for selling. A couple times he began crying and created a really uncomfortable situation for the buyer.

The conclusion for these two examples is obvious – Bill sold his fertilizer company for top dollar and Fred never sold his franchise and still owns them today.

Just like you have a product to sell, you have a business to sell. The principles and practices are no different. You need to rehearse a story that sells your business and be prepared to tell it. Make it interesting but informative and show how your business is unique, fun, and rewarding. Talk about the challenges and show how you overcame them. Tell these stories with a smile on your face and you will get the buyer feeling the sizzle.

Increase your curb appeal

How long has it been since you took a good look at the appearance of your business. Maybe you should take a critical eye and examine what the business looks like. Does it need a new paint job? Is the bathroom clean or does it need new tile? Is the inventory organized, well kept, and neat? Is the paperwork filed? What does your signage look like? If someone came into the office does it look like a tornado just came through the front door?

Now is the time to think of ways to improve the "curb appeal" and make sure the first impression of a buyer is favorable. A buyer is going to value the business less (i.e. lower the price) and struggle to connect with the business if it isn't visually attractive. You would be amazed at how much a first impression will do for the company. In many cases a buyer will determine if they like the company or not in less than 10 minutes of walking around. Make sure you are ready by sprucing up what is needed. This includes getting rid of obsolete inventory, machinery, equipment, furniture, and other fixtures. The business needs to feel clean and crisp and not overwhelmed with stuff.

Compare yourself to the industry

Ask your business broker for information about your industry, competitors, and the market. You should use this information for comparing financial ratios and statistics for your type of business. This information is compiled by multiple sources and readily available. The analysis of the information can be used to make small changes that will be big selling points.

For example, if your industry is turning the inventory every 65 days and you are turning it every 90 days, a buyer will know something isn't right. They will want to dig deeper into the details and will most likely lower the price. On the flip side, if you are producing $1,500,000 in sales with 6 employees and the average company in your industry is doing $1,500,000 in sales with 9 employees, then you can use this metric as a selling point to demonstrate how efficient your operation is compared to others in your industry.

Some of the most common financial metrics include Gross Profit Margin, Net Profit Margin, Inventory Days, Accounts Receivable/Payable Days, etc.

Remember salesmanship is a matter of identifying the positive benefits and features. You need to know what your positives are and how to explain them.

Structuring your business for sale

This is actually a very critical consideration. If you are only 30 days away from listing your business for sale it is probably too late. However, if you are preparing in advance you may want to give some consideration to the type of entity your business is and how to best structure your business for sale.

As business brokers we have a general idea of the best ways to structure your business entity. However, we are not CPA's and we are not estate planning attorneys. You may consider engaging a tax consultant if your situation is somewhat complex. We had a client save roughly $300,000 in taxes by paying a tax consultant $6,500 to review a transaction and make some recommendations.

You may want to consider being a Sub-S Corporation or a Limited Liability Corporation. Maybe you will want a family trust to own the Sub-S and not yourself personally. It may be that you want to have a portion of the proceeds go to your irrevocable trust that has been set up for your children's benefit. You may want to begin gifting a portion of the stock to your children in advance so you can take advantage of the tax gifting laws and avoid personal taxes on the portion you gift.

Whatever the approach, it takes time and some advanced planning. Contact your CPA or engage an estate planning attorney or tax consultant to discuss these matters well in advance of selling your business.

Here is a very important point to remember; we believe that the sale of the business shouldn't be dictated by the tax or accounting laws – the tail wagging the dog. There will be options available for you at any stage of the selling process. It is true that early planning is the best. But keep in mind that if you haven't done all the pre-planning it probably isn't a reason to delay the sale of the business. If now is the right time to sell, then move ahead and make it happen.

Solving business partnership issues

Business partners are either a great blessing or a great curse when it comes to selling your business. You want to make sure that any partner issues have been resolved and that all documentation is in place and signed by all appropriate parties. This is particularly true if there isn't a majority owner in the business. It becomes critical to the success of the sale. The following is an example of a business owner who didn't take care of the issue and it came back to haunt him in the sale of the business.

Jack had run a successful light manufacturing company for over 15 years. He started the company by involving two partners that invested some money. In exchange for the start up money, he gave each of the investors 10% of the company. For 15 years each of the partners received their portion of the profits on a quarterly basis. They quietly received their quarterly distribution check, consistently monitored the company, and assisted Jack in the decision making process. Jack and his two partners made a very lucrative return on the investment.

Jack was ready to sell and move on and do something else. He assumed his partners would approve his decision to sell and moved ahead with the process. He knew he controlled the majority interest in the company anyway. After about 9 months an adequate offer to purchase was made by a qualified buyer. Jack accepted the offer after with some negotiation and committed the company to a sale that would be completed in 30 days.

It was now time to call the investors and make sure they would show up at the closing and collect their check. In this case it was going to be a very sizable check for the two investors. First call went fine. Second call didn't go so well. The investor said he had no intention of selling his 10%. It would create a significant tax consequence for him in the year they were selling and he didn't want to have that happen. He wanted to pass his ownership to his children before the sale to tax reasons. However, there was no enough time to complete the transfer before the agreed upon closing date.

No amount of conversation would change the decision of the investor. The investor realized that if they simply waited another 90 days on the sale it would be a huge difference for him on his taxes and he was pushing to make it happen.

Jack had a problem. He agreed to close the transaction within 30 days and knew the buyer would not wait 90 days. A quick reading of the company by laws revealed that Jack couldn't sell the business without a 100% approval of all stockholders.

I would like to tell you that there was a happy ending to the story but there wasn't. The sale was lost and the investor forced them to wait 90 days. After 90 days another buyer was found but the price had dropped significantly and Jack realized much less cash than he anticipated. Simple preparation would go a long way in solving the problem.

The following is a list of things to consider and address with your partners before engaging in the selling process:

- Will they agree to a sale of the business?
- Is there a buy/sell agreement that specifies how ownership is transferred?
- Can you buy them out in advance?
- Can you sign and obligate them without their approval?
- Are they willing to document that you are authorized to transact the sale?
- Is there a minimum amount they will accept?

These are just a few of the issues you will want to consider. Handle them before you list the company for sale and make sure you and your partners are prepared to sell the business.

Prepare your employees

How to prepare your employees for an ownership transition can be a very sensitive issue. For many business owners the employees are just like family. It is very difficult to leave them with a circumstance that may not be comfortable. How you prepare your employees really comes down to three options discussed below.

Option #1 – Don't tell your employees

Pros

- Business will continue as usual with no interruptions
- Employees will not get nervous and begin to look for other employment
- You will spend less time baby-sitting your employees during the process

31

- The chances of your competitors finding out are significantly reduced
- Your customers have a less likely chance of finding out and thus you won't risk loosing some of your customers in the process.
- If the business doesn't sell you have no backtracking to handle in the process.

Cons

- You run the risk of it leaking out and you will have to do damage control with customers and employees.
- It is difficult to have potential buyers coming and going to see the operation and explain what is happening while keeping it confidential.
- You need to restrict potential buyers with limited access the business.
- The news will come as a complete shock when you announce the business is sold and you will have to deal with those issues all at once.

Option #2 – Tell your employees

Pros

- You can handle the announcement in the way and time you find most appropriate
- You will not have to hide the process
- Buyers will find it much easier to access the business
- Once a buyer is found they can interview and meet with key employees without any restrictions
- Marketing is much easier for the broker and a wider net can be spread to find the right buyer

Cons

- You may have some employees who choose to leave the company and find other jobs before the company sells.
- Vendor, customers, and competition will know and they can use it against you.
- Productivity may decline, as this is a distraction to the normal course of business.

Option #3 – Tell only key employees

Pros

- You can spend time with key employees and reassure them of the outcome and your goals and that you will do all you can to insure a smooth transition.
- It allows potential buyers to visit and meet with key employees in the process.
- Damage control is easier if a problem does arise since you have pre-handled the problem with the key employees.

Cons

- Depending upon the loyalty of the employees they may elect to seek other jobs once they know the company is for sale.
- The more people who know the less likely you can keep the whole process confidential.

We would like to tell you that we know which method is best for your company; the truth is every company, manager, and situation is different. Weigh your options and make the best determination for working with employees. A professional business broker can work within the specification you set for confidentiality and handling employees.

Just as a reference point the majority of businesses elect not to tell employees until they are sure a sale is in place. With that in mind you should know that for every 10 companies that elect not to tell the employees and keep the sale completely confidential, 3 of them would experience a breach of confidentiality. Generally an employee, competitor, vendor, or someone else catches wind of the sale and rumors begin to filter through the system. In many cases it is the owner themselves that can't keep the confidentiality and news spreads. The majority of the time the sale of your business can be made confidential from your employees, vendors, and customers.

Top 10 ways to maximize business value

Everyone seems to have a Top 10 list and here is ours: The top 10 ways to maximize business value and increase personal wealth. Use this list as planning guide and implement changes where appropriate over the long-term. If you are at the doorstep of selling your company then maybe you will only have the time to accomplish a couple of the steps in the process. Even if you have time to accomplish only 1 of the steps you will increase the value and marketability of your company.

The question is why will these things increase the value of my company? The answer is very simple; buyers will pay more for well-prepared business that has established systems, processes, and policies that they know they can just step into and begin running. If they have a hard time learning the operations, obtaining information, understanding policies, or recognizing systems that should be in place, then they will simply walk away from the deal or, even worse, offer a rock bottom price.

One interesting statistic is that 50% of all transactions fail in the due-diligence phase of the selling process. That means that the parties have agreed upon a price, terms and conditions, and have signed agreements to move forward with selling the business. The buyer is then given the time to examine and verify the company records, operations, and assets of the business. During the due diligence review period the buyer can back out of the deal for just about any reason. The most common reason for failure of due diligence is the lack of accurate or complete books and records.

Our top ten list will help you insure that there won't be a problem in the due diligence process. Remember, some of these items may take some serious time and effort. If you are close to a sale then pick the items you can complete. If you still have time before you sell then start on the list now and begin to set aside blocks of time to complete the list. On some topics we have included a brief checklist for that item to insure you are completing the task accurately and completely. A simple to do list for each item will help you start the process and get the work completed.

The top 10 ways to maximize business value and increase personal wealth.

(1) Keep Clean Books and Records

This may sound like a simple task for some business owners and a tedious task for others. But keeping clean books (i.e. Profit and Loss, Balance Sheet, etc.) and records (i.e. Assets Lists, Tax Returns, etc.) can be the difference between having a sellable business or not.

Some business owners are able to do their own books and have an accountant provide Compilation Reports, Reviewed Statements, and sometimes, even Audited Statements. Smaller businesses generally don't manage their business from the financial statements, especially the balance sheet. We understand that. But you should be prepared to present an adequate financial picture for all potential buyers. If this isn't second nature to you, seek the help of a bookkeeper or accountant.

Following is a list of information that is generally required when selling your business:

- Financial statements (P&L, Balance Sheet)
- Tax returns (Form 1120, Schedule C, etc.)
- List of assets to be included in the sale
- List of outstanding debt
- All lease agreements for property, equipment, and vehicles
- All contracts with vendors, customers, and employees
- Copy of the franchise agreement (if applicable)
- Articles of organization and by laws
- Corporate resolution
- Buy sell agreements (if applicable)

- List of owner perks or benefits
- Proof of intellectual property

A potential buyer will examine all of this information during the due diligence phase of the selling process. You should be consistently reviewing this information as good management practice and as part of preparing your business for sale. The most basic of these tasks is to have accurate financial statements. Having the three most recent years of financial statements and the most current interim statements is the starting point for a business valuation, marketing preparation, and information gathering of a buyer.

List of assets to be included in the sale

This isn't as difficult as it may sound. The best place to start is with your tax return. If your CPA prepares your tax return he has probably already accounted for the equipment you can depreciate on your depreciation schedule included in your tax return. It will be on a separate schedule and you can copy that as your starting point. At some point during the selling process you will need to list all the assets that are included in the sale of the business. That would include desks, chairs, computers, copy machines, vehicles, equipment, etc. This is commonly referred to as Furniture, Fixtures, & Equipment or FF&E for short.

At the time of closing the list of assets will be a part of the closing documents so that the buyer knows exactly what they are buying. It also becomes the basis for the purchase price allocation document that both the seller and the buyer will need to determine the tax basis for the transaction. The buyer will be able to claim market value on all the equipment at the time of the close and that allows him to re-depreciate the equipment for tax purposes. Therefore, he has to have the list to complete this accounting exercise.

Sample Asset List

Description	Serial #	Cost	Market Value
HP LaserJet 4300	XNT4567	$350	$150
Roller Chairs Black		$79	$25
Ford F150	28392832	$21,500	$14,290
Racking System 290	TRZ890	$14,250	$11,970
	Total	**$36,179**	**$26,435**

List of outstanding debt

Some of the biggest surprises are with the liabilities of the business. The surprise occurs when an asset cannot pass free and clear to the new owner because of pre-payment penalties or some other restriction associated with the loan on the asset. The seller will be required to sell the assets "free and clear of all liens and encumbrances" in order for the transaction to complete.

The majority of privately held business transactions in the United States are asset sales and not stock sales. The buyer is purchasing the assets of the company, not the company itself. By doing an asset sale the buyer won't inherent the liabilities of your company. Therefore, the assets of the business must past free and clear of all encumbrances to the new owner.

As part of the closing you will have to pay off the debt on all the assets so they can pass free and clear (i.e. no liens against them) to the buyer. That is where this suggestion is critical. You need to make sure that you won't incur penalties by pre-paying the debt. And if you do have pre-payment penalties, you have to be ok with paying them. It isn't uncommon for a lender to include a pre-payment penalty so don't be surprised when you find out one exists. Simply check the documentation or ask the lender if it is the case.

Lease agreements

The two biggest deal killers are lawyers and landlords. Understanding your lease agreement and the options that you have for transferring the lease to the new buyer will be critical to closing the deal. In the event you are leasing your location, the buyer will want some assurance that they can continue that lease with a reasonable term and rate. A business with a great location that contributes to the overall value of the business should always have a long-term lease in place. No buyer wants to buy your business with only 3 months left on the lease and no way of securing the future. We have also seen the opposite scenario happen where the buyer didn't want to be in a long-term lease. This scenario is more common in recessionary times when rent rates are decreasing.

You will need to provide a copy of the lease to the buyer. Often these documents are very long with lots of legal language. It is worth reading so you understand your options. Can you sub-lease to the new buyer and your name stay on the lease? In the event of a transfer of ownership does it require the new owner to qualify for a new lease with new terms and conditions? Can the new owner qualify to assume the lease under the same terms and conditions?

These are questions you will want to know the answers to before you proceed. Generally speaking all leases terminate with the transfer of ownership, however, your obligation to pay the lease may not terminate. It is common practice for the buyer to have a period of time to qualify and/or negotiate a new lease with the landlord.

The most important provisions in the contract are those that outline how the transfer of the lease is to be handle. Often times it is just a matter of getting written approval from the landlord to transfer the lease under the same terms and conditions. Other times, the landlord may require an original lease be drafted with the buyer as the new tenant.

Remember that you are still obligated to pay the lease until the landlord or the lessor releases you. If you let the buyer come in and run your business and they can't make it work after a year and walk away from the business you are stuck on that lease unless you have made arrangements for your release or the buyer has qualified for a new lease. Don't just assume you can transfer the lease.

The same principal applies for equipment leases as does for real estate leases. Take at look at all of them and make sure you have made arrangements for the assumption of the leases, payoffs, or release of liability.

Contracts with vendors, customers

Understanding the terms and conditions of the contracts with your vendors, customers, and employees is all part of a buyers due diligence. Having favorable terms and conditions and provision that allows the contracts to be assigned, or transferred, to a new owner will increase the value of your business and the likelihood of selling the business. Unless you have a written agreement in place that specifies how and when those rights can be transferred it is very difficult to verify for closing. The best place to start is to make sure your agreements are current, signed, and executed properly.

We know of a deal that was at the closing table when it was revealed to the buyer that there was a $30 a month contract in place with a beverage vendor. The buyer was so bugged by this revelation that he walked out of the closing and the transaction came to a screeching stop. A $30 a month contract killed the deal. This is probably the exception rather than the norm. But the lesson learned is the same. Start now by making sure you are prepared with complete and accurate documentation of the contracts and leases by which you are bound.

Human resource files and documentation

Make sure all HR files are accurate and complete. This includes the basic record keeping and employee tracking that each employee should have in his or her own file. By keeping accurate records you will help the buyer avoid problems in the future.

Remember, you will likely sell the business as an asset sale. What this means is all the employees will be terminated the day of the sale and re-hired at the same time by the new entity (Corporation, LLC, etc.) that the buyer has established. If it is a stock sale then the employees will be unaffected and the files and contracts will be in place. Remember all of these files should be under lock and key. Here is a checklist of what should be in each employees human resource file.

- Proof of citizenship
- Signed employee handbook
- Payroll information
- Job description and responsibilities
- Work week and hours
- Safety violations
- Any disciplinary actions
- Annual review sheets
- Benefits description
- Any other vital document concerning employment

Employee agreements

Not all employees will require an employment agreement. In most cases the regular hiring practices and a signed employee handbook will be enough. However, a buyer wants to know if a key employee has an employment agreement and what are the terms and conditions. This may impact the sale and due diligence process.

For example some employment agreements will have a time and compensation mentioned on the term of employment. Many will have a penalty if they leave early. Others will list the possible bonuses or incentives if the employee produces certain goals. All of this type of information for key employees needs to be written down and included in an employment agreement. Doing so will insure that the buyer knows what they have and what they are getting into with their future employees.

List of owner perks and benefits

In order to accurately determine the value of your business, you must know how much money (cash flow) the business can generate. It is not uncommon for business owners to take certain perks from the business that result in lower net income and less taxes being paid. Most of these perks are perfectly legally. But they distort the true amount of money the business generates.

When your business is sold to another person or group they may choose to structure the perks differently or they may have another source that provides the same benefits. For example, some business owners have their companies pay for their medical insurance. Other business owners may have a spouse who works for a different company that provides this benefit. Every case is different. That is why the owner perks are added back to the bottom line cash flow number when determining the value of a business.

You will certainly increase the value of the business by documenting perks or personal expenses that you run through the company. To help you think through all the areas that you may have perks or expenses here is a list of some of the most common items.

- Life insurance paid on the owner
- Health insurance paid on the owner
- Cell phone bills
- Car payments
- Gasoline expense
- Meals and entertainment for owner
- Rent paid to the owner
- Lease payments paid to owner

- Personal credit cards bills paid for owner
- Auto insurance
- Personal items purchased through the business such as groceries
- Personal travel paid by company

Document employee benefit programs

Do you have a 401k plan, health plan, dental plan, life insurance, or maybe even an ESOP (Employee stock option plan). If so, you need to make sure they are well documented, signed be each employee that is participating in the plan, and included in each employees file.

This is particularly important for companies that have multiple employees on different plans based upon the conditions of their employment – length of employment, type of work, and pay level. All of these issues need to be considered and documented.

Consider the following situation. Prior to closing Matt wasn't sure what his company had done with all the 401k obligations and benefit programs for each of his 35 employees. He knew his human resource manager took care of the issues but he wasn't current on the status. As closing drew near the buyer began investigating the obligation associated with each of the plans. To Matt's surprise the company had not made the matching 401k contributions for a number of employees. It resulted in a $21,000 dollar adjustment to the purchase price because the matter wasn't handled and Matt had to make those contributions at closing.

Make the time to put all of the terms and conditions for each of your benefit programs in writing (they should be in your employee handbook as a standard practice). Also make sure you are fully funded on all obligations for the benefit programs. Again, window dressing is important. A buyer wants a clean well run company.

Compile corporate entity and partnership agreements

Compiling the corporate entity and partnership agreements should have happened when you created the company. If you had an attorney organize the company then chances are you have this documentation. If you organized the company yourself then you need to insure that you have the documentation on record and can provide it when it is requested.

There are different types of business entities and each type requires certain documents to insure your status with the state and federal government are current and in good standing. The easiest solution is to first check with the secretary of state to insure that your company is in good standing with the state and you have filed all required documents. Next get all of your legal documents together and pay for an easy and inexpensive review by your attorney. Additionally most states require you to hold at least annual member or shareholder meetings and record those meetings in writing. Keeping clean documents will be helpful at the time of sale especially if the buyer is purchasing the stock or member shares.

The most common corporate entity filings are the Articles of Incorporation/Organization. The By Laws to the Articles of Organization are not public record but should be prepared and made available as needed. Buy/Sell Agreements describe how ownership is to be bought and sold amongst the owners/partners of the business. The notes from the Annual Board Meetings with any decisions that were made are also part of this information. The Shareholders ledger should contain information about the stock ownership of the company.

Proof of intellectual property

Many businesses have customized software, specialized services, or proprietary processes referred to trade secrets or intellectual property. Laws can protect some of this information.

But most of this information is just the way the owner does business that makes them successful. Let me give you an example.

A local agricultural company had spent years refining their system for producing and mixing the perfect seed combination for farmers. A group of employees had over time develop specialized systems for insuring that just the right amount of seed and the correct amount of additives were in each batch sold to farmers. It was obviously working because the company had garnered a very loyal following and the company was growing as a result.

The system was a combination of four processes and a different employee in a different part of the building completed each process. The company had never taken the time to document the process. It didn't take long for the owner to realize that if he sold the company and any of those employees left he would have a problem maintaining the same standard of product. With a little bit of time and effort this process was documented and preserved for the next business owner.

Take the time to examine what your company has and/or does that may require special documentation to insure it is transferable with a sale. Be specific and detailed. It will go a long way to insuring a buyer you are prepared to transfer the valuable assets of the company.

(2) Maximize Sales and Profits

If you want to truly maximize the value of your business, then you need to be focused on increasing sales and maximizing profits. Let's take a look at why this is important.

First, consider what a buyer is really buying. A buyer is really buying a stream of cash – also called the profits, cash flow, or sellers discretionary earnings. Buyers are willing to pay an amount of money for the future rights to that cash flow so long as it provides a return on their investment. Don't make the mistake of some business owners who believe they are selling assets. The reality is they are selling the future rights to the cash flow generated by those assets.

Second, consider how the asking price for a business is determined. The most widely accepted methodology for business brokers in determining the value of business to be bought or sold is the Multiple of Seller's Discretionary Earnings method. We discuss this topic at length later in the book. So for now, all you need to know is that a number is selected – called a multiplier – and multiplied by cash flow to determine the value of the business.

Third, a business with steadily increasing sales and profits is more desirable then one that fluctuates dramatically year-to-year. Take a look at the following examples:

Example #1

	Earnings
Year 1	$ 450,000
Year 2	$75,000
Year 3	$ 185,000
3-Year Average	$ 236,666

Example #2

	Earnings
Year 1	$75,000
Year 2	$ 185,000
Year 3	$ 450,000
3-Year Average	$ 236,666

The "3-Year Average" for both examples is identical. Now lets' assume that after researching the market data we determine the cash flow multiplier for this business is 2.45. Example #1 will have a sales price of $464,275 and Example #2 will have a sale price of $880,775. That is a HUGE difference of $416,500. The owner of the business in Example #2 had consistently grown the business profits for three years.

You might be asking yourself why such a difference. The answer is the most recent years performance will be weighted higher then the previous years. For businesses that have fluctuating profits the 70/20/10 principal will be applied to the cash flow. That means that Year 3 cash flow is valued at 70%, Year 2 at 20%, and Year 1 at 10%. The result of steadily growing sales and profits is a higher business valuation.

One other key point is to report all income earned by the business. This is especially true in the 3 to 5 years prior to selling your business. What causes a business owner to not report all their income? The answer is the IRS. Nobody likes to pay taxes and so we try and find ways to drive the net income number down and thereby reducing the amount of taxes we pay. This approach is just fine until we come to the point of selling your business.

A business that reports all their income and pays taxes will be worth more than the business that did not. We call this investing in taxes. Take a look at the scenario below:

	A	B
Sales	$500,000	$500,000
Unreported		**$(100,000)**
Expenses	$(300,000)	$(300,000)
Net Income (Discretionary Earnings)	$200,000	$100,000
Multiple	2.45	2.45
Value	$490,000	$245,000
Taxes Paid	$(80,000)	$(40,000)
Proceeds to Seller	$410,000	$205,000

Business A reported all of their income and paid $80,000 in taxes. Business B chose to not report $100,000 of their income. The result was they saved $40,000 in taxes. However, when it came to value the business, A was worth 2 times as much as B. Report all income, invest in taxes, and your business will sell for a higher price in the long run.

Hopefully we have encourage you to focus and maximizing your sales and profits, reporting all income generated by the business even if it means paying higher taxes, and steadily growing your company 3 to 5 years before you decide to sell the business. All of these steps will help you successfully transfer business ownership.

Analyze Industry Standards

Not many business owners have access to industry standard data for financial ratios and production. This information can be extremely valuable and a critical component in preparing your business for sale. A number of companies have taken the time to compile all the data necessary to compare your company to other companies just like yours in your industry. For example if you run a sporting goods store, there is data on what the average sporting goods store does in the form of financial ratios and production. It may be hard for you to track down this information and it may be expensive; however, a quality business broker will have access to this type of information and should be willing to provide the information for you at no cost.

You will find valuable information on how your company stacks up to all your competitors. You may find out some interesting information about inventory turns, accounts receivable days, profit margins, and much more. Below is a list of the most common metrics for comparing your business to your competitors.

- Current financial ratio
- Quick financial ratio
- Inventory days average
- Accounts receivable days average
- Accounts payable days average
- Average Gross Margin
- Average Net Margin
- Rent to sales
- Payroll to sales
- Debt ratios
- Return on equity
- Return on assets

By looking at what your competitors are doing you can see where your business has strengths and weaknesses. For example, if the industry average of payroll to sales is much higher in your business than everyone in your industry, then you may want to look closer at your employees and consider making some changes – downsizing, retraining, etc. If the industry is collecting their accounts receivable 15 days faster on average than you are, then you may want to consider changing your terms, offering incentives for early payment, or charging a penalty for paying late.

You will increase the value of your business by running some numbers, doing a little analysis, and comparing your business to others in the industry. Your business will also show better on paper to attract the attention of qualified buyers. The only thing better than a qualified buyer is many qualified buyers who are bidding on your company and driving the price up.

Review Your Pricing Structure

If you don't check your pricing, the buyer will. Almost all buyers will take the time to shop the competition before they buy a company. There are many ways to go about this process. If the pricing of your competitors is easy to find, then it isn't a problem. Be very thorough and complete in your price checks. Find as many identical and matching products and services as possible and price them at various quantities to make sure you understand their quantity breaks.

The exercise of reviewing your competitors prices becomes difficult if they are a guarded and keep secret. You may consider a professional shopping firm. They will go into your competitor undetected and price all the products you request and simply report back to your for a fee. Another option is to ask your vendors. They may readily give this information without hesitation.

Keep in mind that pricing your competition has nothing to do with where you price your products and services. You may elect to raise your prices or lower your prices. Companies carve out successful niches by being the high-end player, the low price player, or the middle of the market player. Whatever strategy you are employing is fine, you just need to be aware of your competition pricing so that a buyer who wants an explanation of why you are 45% higher on your two lowest moving products does not catch you off guard.

(3) Polish Your Image

Polish your image, increase your curb appeal, and keep your business clean, functional, and organized. No buyer will buy your business until they have come to see the operations and the location. This is a critical step in having the buyer be emotionally connected to the business. Nothing will cause a buyer to hesitate more than a poor first impression. A perfect example of this happened about two years ago.

Dave was a busy business owner that had been in the same location for over 15 years. In those 15 years he had not changed one thing in the business office or storefront. It came time to sell and we pleaded with Dave to spruce the place up a bit. Dave had a very unique niche and one of a kind operation that few buyers would find attractive and it would be a difficult sale because the pool of buyers with the expertise to operate the business was very small.

After months of work a buyer emerged that was qualified, willing, and determined to buy the business. They buyer analyzed the numbers, asked probing questions, and was ready to visit the business and meet the seller in person. The big day come and Dave was just too busy to make many changes to the appearance of the office.

When the buyer showed up it was obvious he was not impressed with what he saw. To make matter worse, the buyer brought his wife along for the tour. About 20 minutes into the tour she asked to use the bathroom. Unfortunately no one had cleaned the office bathroom in sometime and the toilet was clogged. She went in the bathroom and immediately came back out.

She quietly told her husband that they needed to leave and that this wasn't the right business for them. The sale was lost. We could never get the buyer to overcome the fact his wife had been disgusted by the bathroom. The appearance of the business ruined what could have been a good deal.

Take the time to look at what needs cleaned, painted, fixed, moved around, swapped out, relocated, and repaired. Put your best foot forward. Show that you are organized, clean, and professional

(4) Manage Your Customer List

Perhaps the most valuable of all the intangible assets is the customer list. For most businesses, the value of the customers is the largest part of the goodwill. Any strategic buyer that wants to increase market share will be mostly interested in who your customers are and how much they can add to the bottom line profits. The value of the customer list is significant.

In our experience, small business owners poorly manage their customer list and don't spend enough time or resources selling additional products and services to their existing customers. For whatever reason, they always seem to be focused on getting that next new customer. There is plenty of evidence to support the fact that the cost of a sale to a new customer far exceeds the cost of a sale to an existing customer.

We were surprised to find out that one of our past clients didn't have one bit of information on any of his customers. He owned a rock quarry that provided some of the most beautiful granite pavers, countertops, mantles, and markers. His customers included landscapers, builders, and individuals that would likely buy again and again. He could have easily collected their contact information at the time of the sale. With that information he could do direct mailers, special promotions, surveys, and postcards to remind his customers to buy more product.

You should have some kind of marketing effort and incentives to learn more about your customers and their buying habits. Conduct online surveys to find out what your customers need and want. Send them promotions and coupons with special offers for being loyal customers. Consider having a customer appreciation event to again solidify that relationship and create happy and loyal customers.

If you don't have a system for managing your customer list, get one right now. There is an abundance of software and technology to support your effort. Most financial software systems have the ability to track customer information. A number of Customer Relationship Management (CRM) tools also exist that take tracking customer information one step further into promoting that relationship through automation. It will be a great selling point to any potential buyer if your customer list is current, clean, and active.

(5) Control Inventory

Managing inventory seems like a basic business school topic. However, anyone that has ever tried to efficiently manage inventory knows can be extremely challenging. Purchasing, tracking, and adjusting inventory is a time consuming process that is part science and part art. You purchase too much and end up with obsolete, damaged, outdated goods. If you loose track of the inventory and cannot effectively monitor where goods are and where they are going, then somehow the goods grow feet and disappear. Then there is the annual inventory count for the purpose of adjusting what you have on your books with what you actually have. Not a fun task for most business owners.

Annual inventory checks inventory checks are fine if you have a system in place for managing your inventory. The problem comes when you don't have a regular system in place for checking your inventory and you haven't made the necessary adjustments for obsolete, damaged, or outdated inventory.

The inventory is a tangible asset just like the furniture, fixtures, equipment, or real estate. What makes the inventory different is that the value is constantly changing. If the inventory is included in the asking price, then the asking price technically always

53

changing. For this reason, when a buyer makes an offer on the business, the offer price will include a snapshot of the inventory at the time when the offer was made. When the business sales, another snapshot will be taken of the inventory at that time. An adjustment will be made, either up or down, to the purchase price to account for the change in inventory offer time.

Keep in mind that any business sale where the inventory is included as one of the assets will likely include an inventory adjustment at closing. Generally buyers want to know that the value stated on the balance sheet for the inventory is the actual value. It is not unusual for an inventory to be off by $1,000's and sometimes $10,000's of dollars. Therefore it will likely be counted just before the closing. You don't want any surprises at that time. If you stated the inventory at $732,000, then it needs to be very close to that number. Any differences in the number will mean that the sales price is adjusted. For example if the pricing of the business is based upon an inventory level of $730,000 and the actual counting of the inventory revealed that the true value of the inventory is $700,000 then the sales price will be adjusted down by $30,000 to reflect the accurate inventory level.

Some business owners just can't bring themselves to get rid of any inventory no matter how obsolete, damaged, or outdated the inventory is. The CEO of one of the largest grocery stores in the country could not understand that keeping this inventory in the stores and on the books was costing the company thousand of dollars. He even went so far as to suggest a marketing campaign to clear out old merchandise left offer from the holidays – he called it Christmas in July. What he didn't understand was the cost of this old inventory was never going to be recovered. They would have been better off throwing the merchandise in the garbage. When dealing with inventory, your first loss is your best loss. Get rid of it and move on.

A final consideration on the topic of inventory is the method by which you count the inventory. The two most common methods are FIFO (first in first out) and LIFO (last in first out). Because the cost of your inventory varies over time, you need to be familiar with the method you are using. If the method changes at some point, it will impact the value of your inventory stated on the balance sheet. This is good topic to discuss with your accountant.

(6) Manage Receivables

Just like inventory, the management of your accounts receivable is a key indicator that will separate a sellable business from one that is not. To take it one step further, great businesses are distinguished from average businesses by their ability to collect payment for their products and services. A buyer will want to analyze bad debts or uncollected accounts receivable. They will also want to analyze the accounts receivable aging report to understand the accounts receivable days average. This is an important ratio for maintaining the liquidity of a business.

Most business transactions are structured as asset sales and not stock sales. What that means is the seller is going to keep the accounts receivable and collect them after the sale. The accounts receivable become less of an issue for the buyer because they don't receive them anyway. The buyer will begin to establish their own accounts receivable after the sale from goods and service they are responsible for selling. Because the buyer isn't worried about collecting the sellers accounts receivable, he doesn't care if you collect them or write them off – that is your decision.

If the sale of your company is a stock sale then the accounts receivable will be a part of the sale and will transfer to the new owner. This is where it becomes important to know the collectable portion of your accounts receivable and to write off any portion that is uncollectible. If the industry standard for collecting your accounts receivable is 35 days and you have $35,000 of accounts receivable that are 120 days past due, the buyer will not include those in the sale and the money received for your business will be reduced accordingly. The collectability of these accounts always becomes a sticking point and a matter of negotiation. How you manager accounts receivable is another good topic to discuss with your accountant.

(7) Manage Payables

One of the biggest deal killers is surprise. Buyers are especially uncomfortable with anything that catches them off guard. Most financial accounting software can handle accounts payable and provide reports for analyzing this important part of your business. Share this information with potential buyers and help them understand how payables are managed in your business.

In an asset sale you will most likely be required to pay off all of your accounts payable at closing or within 30 days after closing. It is very unusual in an asset sale for the buyer to assume any liabilities. What usually happens is the escrow company will use the proceeds from the sale at closing to pay off the accounts payable so the buyer can step into the business with a clean slate, free from the past owners liabilities.

A stock sale is different. The buyer will be assuming the liabilities of the company and will be responsible to pay the accounts payable starting the day after the transaction closes. Just prior to the closing date a *working capital adjustment* may be made to account for the changes during the time period with the offer was made and the deal was closed.

In both scenarios – asset sale or stock sale – the accounts payable need to be well documented, organized, and current. Avoid the element of surprise when managing payables.

(8) Review Your Product Mix

This seems very intuitive but for most business owners it becomes hard to part with product lines or services that have been around for a long time or that maybe the owner has nurtured and grown over the years. The first step in this process is to determine if a product line is profitable or if it is loosing money. The second step is to determine if an unprofitable product line is supporting other lines. There are other consideration such as the impact a product line with have on your marketing plans or ability to qualify for certain incentives on those product lines. The third step is to determine how to effectively discontinue the line if that is the best course to pursue.

One of the key elements for maximizing business value is having strong profits. If you have an unproductive line, then it is most likely eating into your cash flow and reducing your profits. That will drive down the value of the company. In an upcoming chapter of this book you are going to be given some extensive information on how the value of your business is determined.

The "dead wood" of an unproductive product line will not impress a buyer. If the buyers can quickly determine that you have unproductive lines, it may be easier for them to just move on to the next option rather than work through the process of correcting the product line balance. Now would be the best time to do the analysis, make the hard decisions and correct the unproductive lines.

(9) Develop a Skilled Management Team

Some business owners are involved in every aspect of their business – the day-to-day operations, management and supervision, financial decision-making, strategy planning, etc. If they aren't working, then the business comes to a halt. They have a hard time stepping away from the business to go on vacation or take time off. This type of scenario is not good for the owners and will limit the number of options they have when it comes time to sell the business.

The best businesses are those where a strong management team exists with the skills and knowledge to run the business in the absence of the owners. Even better is a business where the individual roles are so clearly defined that it doesn't matter who is in the role the job still gets done. This may be impossible for jobs requiring skilled labor and technical expertise. But for a frontline staff worker, anybody should be able to step in and complete the work.

Buyers want to see loyal employees with a solid track record. They want to see a management team that can keep the business going through the transition from the seller to the buyer. If the buyer has to recruit new management this will reduce the value of the business and cause delays in the acquisition.

If the buyer is a private equity group or other strategic buyer, they often rely on the current management as part of their acquisition strategy. In fact, they won't even consider an acquisition if the management team isn't willing to stay on and continuing running the business. This may include a limited role for the sellers of the business over a one or two year period. If you want to attract investors, venture capitalists, private equity groups, start now to develop your management team.

(10) Create an Operations Manual

This is probably the most difficult task in the list. It requires time and effort and may feel like tedious busy work. As mentioned before, many business owners spend all of their time working *in* the business and not *on* the business. This is a perfect opportunity to work *on* the business.

Some businesses function purely on the knowledge and expertise of the owner and a few key employees. If the owner of the business were to go away – and they do when a business is sold – no one would have an idea of how things are run or what the company policies and procedures entail. A buyer wants to see an operations manual to help minimize that risk.

Your operations manual could take the form of standard operating procedures (SOP) or just a list of best practices. Once you have documented your operations you should update them when a change is made. It may be helpful to schedule a period review to keep things up-to-date. An operations manual is a great tool for training new employees and creating accountability for your existing employees. If they do something wrong and don't follow the established policies or processes, you can simply refer them to the operations manual and take necessary action.

An operations manual is a good selling point that will separate your business from the rest. A potential buyer will be assured that they can come in and run the business in the absence of a key employee or the previous owner. From a marketing perspective, if the business broker can include the fact that the company has a complete operations manual it is a great bonus for generating interest in the company. It is hard to place a value on the operations manual other than to say it makes the business more appealing that a buyer will find a greater willingness to purchase a business knowing that the day after they close, no matter what happens to the seller, the majority of the company processes, policies, and procedures are documented.

Chapter 3 – Working with a Business Broker

You will have to evaluate the idea of hiring a business broker to represent you and manage the selling process or to manage the process yourself. The information that follows will give you some idea of how business brokers work, what services they provide, and how to find a broker that can serve you the best. To be fair we should remind you that we are business brokers and may be a little biased on this topic. You may be surprised when you read this section about some of the views and advice we have regarding this issue.

If your business is worth less than $100,000 you may be able to sell the business yourself and avoid paying a commission to a business broker. If your business is worth more than $250,000, it is likely you will need the services of a business broker to determine the business value, identify and qualify buyers, and manage the process of transferring ownership professionally and legally.

Deciding whether to use a business broker is based upon two key issues:

1. The type of business you own
2. Who you want to manage the selling process

Understanding the type of businesses you own

Before we get started you need to understand what type of business you own. Privately held companies' represent 90% of all businesses in the United States. Privately held companies' are owned by individuals, partnerships, or private equity groups. The ownership, or stock, is not publicly traded or sold on the open market such as the New York Stock Exchange.

Most privately held business transactions are *asset sales* rather than *stock sales*. Meaning that the assets of the company are sold to another entity leaving behind a "shell" company. We will discuss this topic in a later chapter. How you approach selling your business will be based largely on its size and the kind of buyer that will be interested in your acquiring your type of business.

Understanding the types of Business Brokers

Let's discuss the decision of hiring a qualified business broker or intermediary or selling the business by your self. Much of this decision may revolve around the size, industry, and complexity of the business you intend to sell. There are three broad categories of businesses brokers – also called intermediaries – that you will hear referred to as Main Street Business Brokers, Mid-Market Business Brokers, and Merger & Acquisition Advisors.

Main Street Business Broker

The first category is the Main Street Business Broker. Brokers in this category normally sell businesses worth less than $1,000,000. Far and away the largest number of businesses in the United States falls into this category. The Main Street Business Broker will list as many businesses as possible to attract as many buyers as possible. Odds are that with enough buyers a match will be found and the business will be sold.

Mid-Market Business Broker or Intermediary

The second category is the Mid-Market Business Broker or Intermediary. Businesses in this category are worth more than $1,000,000, may have complex business models, would potentially attract partnerships and private equity groups as buyers, and will certainly need the services of a professional business broker or intermediary to attract buyers and manage the process. In this category a professional advisor will manage the details of the process and complexities of the transaction that can be difficult to understand and cumbersome for the business owner.

Mid-Market Business Brokers will limit the number of listings and carefully target potential buyers. They may require a retainer up front for their services in addition to a commission or success fee.

Mergers & Acquisitions Advisors

The Mergers & Acquisitions Advisors are hired as a team and work more like consultants charging hourly fees in addition to commissions. Many regional and national business consulting firms have an M&A practice that are part of the services they provide. Investment banking firms will also offer M&A services.

An M&A Advisor will attract private equity groups, strategic buyers, and potentially organize public offerings. Large companies worth more than $10,000,000 in value with complex issues should consider hiring a team of professionals including accountants and attorneys. Often an M&A Advisors provides all of the expertise needed to complete a large transaction that is complex.

Managing the selling process

Next is deciding who will manage the process of selling the business. You can certainly attempt to sell the business by yourself and avoid paying a commission to a business broker. A better alternative is to hire a professional business broker that is familiar with the process and has the skills, knowledge, and experience to make the transition as smooth as possible. To make this simple lets spell out the benefits and concerns of each option.

Hire a Business Broker

<u>Benefits</u>

- Business brokers can maintain confidentiality.
- Business brokers understand the selling process and can avoid costly mistakes.
- You can continue to operate the business without being distracted with an additional task of selling your business.
- Business brokers are skilled negotiators and will get a higher price for your business.
- Business brokers can advertise your business and attract qualified buyers without appearing desperate to sell.
- Business brokers has the necessary legal forms and documents to transfer ownership legally.

<u>Concerns</u>

You will pay a 10% to 15% commission for a business broker to sell your business.

Sell Your Business Yourself

Benefits

- You won't have to pay a commission for the transaction.
- You control the process and timeline.
- You deal with every aspect of the transaction.

Concerns

- You won't be able to maintain confidentiality.
- You must handle preparing the sales offering.
- You must handle the marketing.
- You will have to screen all calls and inquiries.
- You will have a "to do" list for every interested buyer.
- You will have to coordinate the work of an attorney and accountant.
- You are responsible for making sure terms and conditions are met.
- You will still have to run your business.

The size of your company is an issue when it comes to determining if you need a business broker. Let's give you two extremes.

We have a friend named Joe that left college and had a difficult time landing a job in his chosen field of broadcasting. After a while money became tight. So in order to survive he started washing windows for commercial businesses – the same job that put him through school. Joe realized that washing windows full-time he could make $30,000 a year. He established a number of significant commercial accounts that liked his work and consistently paid.

Finally Joe was offered a job as a sportscaster at a local TV station. He jumped at the opportunity. Joe needed to sell the business as quickly as possible. He figured it was probably worth about $15,000 dollars. He ran an ad in the local paper and had three calls. One of the three interested parties followed him around at work a few days and then offered to give him $5,000 a month for 3 months. They struck the deal and put it in writing. The business was sold and Joe moved on to the next phase of his life.

It is obvious that this transaction was relatively small and not very complicated. He had no employees, no real estate, no inventory, no accounts receivable, and no significant legal documentation to make sale legitimate. Joe easily completed this transaction by himself without the services of a business broker.

In our other example, Tom had $5,000,0000 business with 30 employees, 4 locations, and a complex product. He was 64 years old and wanted to retire. He knew that his business was sellable, but he had now idea how to find a buyer that could purchase a business this size or understood the product well enough to be successful.

Tom hired a business broker and sold his business for top dollar. The business broker was paid a $350,000 commission for completing the job. As the Tom and the Broker were walking out of the closing, Tom told the broker that he had earned every penny of his commission. Tom realized that the broker was able to get a higher price, was able to structure significant tax savings, and was able to manage the process professionally and legally. All of this added up to way more than the broker's commission. It was money well spent by smart business owner

As a general rule of thumb, if your business is valued less than a $100,000, you many not need a business broker to handle the transaction. If the business is more than $100,000 but less than $250,000, you understand the process, and you have some trusted advisors in the form of attorney and CPA, then you may elect to sell your business yourself. If the business is valued at over $250,000 you will probably need to consider a business broker to find a buyer and walk you through the process.

One of the easiest ways to determine if you need a business broker is to complete reading chapter 5 of this book. It covers the steps in selling a business. After reading that chapter if you are confident that you can successfully complete all of those steps on your own then maybe you don't need a business broker. If those steps seem overwhelming, complex, or just too time-consuming, then you probably need a business broker.

There are many factors to consider in this process; however, a few key factors should help you understand what advantages and disadvantages a business broker provides.

Focus on running your business

Most business owners are actively involved in running their business. The last thing they need is one more thing to worry about. There is a significant amount of time spent preparing the company for sale including developing marketing materials, managing advertising, finding and qualifying buyers, exchanging information with potential buyers and answering questions, preparing financial documents and closing documents, coordinating meetings, and overall supervising the selling process. A business broker will handle all of these tasks for you so you can focus on running your business.

We have seen it happen more then once that a business owner becomes too involved with the selling process and diverts their efforts away from running their business. The result is almost always negative. Sales slip, profits shrink, employee's get suspicious and unmotivated, and the business slides into the category of under performing. The business owner needs to continue running the business as if they were going to own it forever.

Have skilled negotiator structure the deal

There is some real value in having a third party negotiate the deal. Perhaps the most effective negotiating tool is "the appeal to a higher authority." A business broker acting as a buffer between the buyer and seller can always say to the buyer, "I need to check with the seller to see if they will agree to that." That allows them to come back to the seller, discuss the terms and conditions, and re-approach the buyer.

A business broker can push harder on price and terms. They can also provide creative solutions for difficult transactions. Often the business owner is too emotionally tied to their company to think rationally and practically about the situation and there comes a time when the seller has to think like a buyer and vice versa. This level of understanding between the parties is critical to reaching the magic "meeting of the minds." The business brokers role is to facilitate this process while managing everyone's expectations.

Leverage the knowledge and experience

Most seasoned business brokers have seen a lot of transactions and know exactly what to expect and how to handle the process. For example, will you know the difference between a stock sale price and an asset sale price? Will you know how to allocate purchase price when it comes to closing? Have you ever heard of someone purchasing your business by using their 401K? Do you know how to handle confidential issues and pre-qualify the buyers? The list goes on and on. Using a business broker allows you to call on years of experience and knowledge to handle all of the possible situations that could come up in the process.

Find and qualify potential buyers

How are you going to market your business once it is time to sell? Do you know where to get the best exposure, how to find the best buyers, and how to effectively handle all the issues associated with confidentiality and marketing? Business brokers can handle these issues. A quality business broker will already have a number of buyers in their database. These are companies and individuals they have worked with a number of times who are interested in buying companies and have provided some basic information to the broker. Also, business brokers will belong to most of the major multiple listing services for business and have access for marketing exposure. Additionally, business brokers will target strategic buyers for your business and will likely do a mailing or phone campaign to find strategic buyers (companies in your industry or like-industries that will have an interest in expanding).

Assemble a team of experts

A business broker will have connections and work with specialized accounting firms, tax attorneys, estate planners, bankers, specialized financial services, etc. All of which they can call on if the complexity of the transactions requires such relationships to be used. These are usually tried and true professionals who have experience in handling specialized situations.

If you have made the decision to use a business broker then there is a logical second step and that is how to find the right business broker.

Find the right business broker

Choosing the right business broker can make or break your chances at success. This will likely be the largest financial decision you will make in your life and certainly you can spend some time finding the best match for your personality, for your company, and for success. Here are a few factors to consider.

Experience

This is a rather obvious criterion. You don't want a business broker that is new, never been in the industry, or has very little if any real experience. Again, ask how long they have been in the industry and what types of businesses they have worked with in the process.

Industry specifications

Brokers can sell almost any type of business in just about every industry. Most business brokers have worked with a large cross-section of business industries and have been exposed to the differences of each. The approach to selling your business does not change dramatically between industries. Unless you are selling a highly specialized business that requires specific licensing (i.e. veterinarian hospital), who you choose doesn't matter except for one thing. Brokers that have worked in the same industry for a long time will know who the buyers are and will have the ability to attract the best buyer for your business. For the most part, brokers can handle your specific industry and needs.

Personality

Your business broker needs to be a person that you can create a strong working relationship with as the process proceeds. Make sure they have a personality that you are comfortable working with. You will be spending time working with them, trusting them, and paying them. In every transaction there are ups and downs. At times you will wonder why it is so difficult to sell a company, during those times you need to be sure you have the right business broker and you can work through problems with them and their personality. They need to be educated, responsive to your needs, trustworthy, and professional.

How much will a business broker charge?

This question is very difficult to answer. There are laws that prohibit business brokers from colluding to charge a certain fee. However, from experience working with a broad range of brokers, the commission for transactions less than a million dollars fall in the range of 8 to 12 percent of the purchase price. For transactions over a million dollars, the commission is based on a declining scale starting at 10 percent.

Almost for every business broker there is a different pricing structure. The information provided in this section is only meant as a general outline. Your case and your situation may be different.

Business brokers fall into three different compensation models:

Commission Only

The majority of business brokers work on a success fee or commission. That means they are only paid if they sell your business. They are generally paid a percentage of the full purchase price. The fee charged is different for every business broker and for every transaction. For transactions less than a million dollars, the commission ranges from 8 to 12 percent of the purchase price. For transactions over a million dollars, the commission is based on a declining scale starting at 10 percent.

Retainer plus Commission

Some brokers require a small retainer for their work in addition to a commission. In these cases, the broker will reduce the commission if a retainer is paid upfront. The overall amount of money paid by the seller to the broker will be less. Many business owners are skeptical about this type of arrangement fearing that their business will never sale and that the retainer money was wasted. This may happen. However, if you have a sellable business and are confident that a transaction can be completed, you may want to seriously consider this option.

From our perspective there are three good things that will happen from paying a retainer upfront and a lesser commission on the back end. First, the broker will know that you are motivated to sell the business and they will be more likely to want to represent your company (no broker wants to represent a business that can't be sold). Second, the broker will have additional money to package and market the business to find the best buyer for your business. And lastly, you will save a significant amount of money on the reduced commission. In our practice we find that about half the sellers opt for paying a retainer for a smaller commission later and the other half elect to work on a commission only basis with a slightly higher rate.

Fee for Services

There are still some brokers who simply charge a "Fee for Service." This is a flat fee or hourly fee for the work performed no matter the outcome or success of the transaction. Not many of these brokers are still around, but there are a few. This may be of interest to you if you already have the buyer and just need someone to help you through the details of the transaction and closing.

When visiting with your business broker and before you sign any agreement make sure you fully understand the fees and commissions and how they will be paid. There are always costs associated with marketing and closing a transaction. Make sure you are clear on who covers those costs along with the commission and retainers charged.

Business Broker Representation Agreement

Again we can only talk in generalities when it comes to representation agreements because every firm will have a slightly different contract. However, there are some elements that all brokers are required by law to include on their contract. Below are some of the most common provisions in the listing agreement.

The Agreement Must be in Writing

In order for any representation agreement to be legally enforced it must be in writing and signed and dated by both parties.

Agency Representation

The contract must clearly state the type of agency representation. The topic of agency representation could be a book by itself. The most common types of agency include Non-Agency, Agency Representation, Limited Dual Agency Representation, and Limited Dual Agency with Assigned Agents. The most common relationship for business sales is when the seller grants the right to the business brokers to exclusively sell their business and act as their agent. You will see this as an "exclusive right to sell." Be sure you understand agency before signing any listing agreement.

Term of the Agreement

The contract must have certain beginning and ending, or expiration, date. Typically, business broker representation agreements are for a period of 12 months. This may seem like a long time, but remember it takes on average 9 months for a typical mid-market business to sell.

Description of Property or Business

In order for the agreement to be enforceable there must be an accurate description of the business and the assets that will be sold as part of the sale. The agreement must clearly indicate if the real property (real estate), inventory, accounts receivable, furniture, fixtures, and equipment along with all other intangible assets are included. In some states, the legal description of the property must be included as well.

It is likely that things will change from the time the business is listed for sale and the time the business is actually sold. That is ok. Part of the process is structuring the deal to make the most sense for both the seller and the buyer. And more often then not, the specifics stated on the listing agreement will be different then the ones that close the deal.

Price and Terms

The agreement must include the price be offered and the acceptable terms and conditions. This information becomes the target that you and the broker are shooting for knowing that it most likely will change. Now it rarely happens that you get exactly the price you wanted for your business or the terms and conditions. Our experience has been that both parties have to make some concessions to successfully transfer business ownership.

All Fees and Commissions

Early in this chapter we talked about how business brokers are paid. Whatever the arrangement is between you and your broker, it should be clearly defined in the listing agreement. Any fees or commissions should be described along with the manner by which the fees and commissions will be paid – upfront, at closing, monthly, etc. You should be aware that commissions are negotiable and not fixed. You should also be aware that business brokers are savvy negotiators and generally unwilling to back down from their standard fees.

Signature of the Owner or Representative

Once again, in order for an agreement to be enforceable, the business owner or their representative must sign. Some business owners may draft a Corporate Resolution document that designates one person to act on behalf of the company and its shareholder. This is a convenience for the business owners when it comes to listing the business, negotiating offers, and signing the closing documents. It is not required to have a corporate resolution.

We have provided a sample listing agreement in the appendix of this book for your review and consideration.

Chapter 4 – Determining Business Value

A study was conducted several years ago to understand small businesses in America. Among the many facts that were discovered were that 80% of the entrepreneur's net worth is tied up in privately owned business and 75% of business owners had no idea how they would exit their business. That is very reflective of what we have found during our years of experience.

The single biggest investment for most business owners is the equity they have in their own business. This is not exactly a model for mitigating risk through diversification. And to make matters worse, small business owners have no idea how to capitalize on this investment by converting that equity to cash.

It would seem then, that knowing the value of your business would be an important issue for small business owners. Unfortunately, it is not. One explanation may be that small business owners do not understand business valuation or how to measure the value. The information that follows will help you determine business value and create a way for monitoring and analyzing the ups and downs or your business.

What is Value?

It is not uncommon for a business owner to think their business is worth more and a potential buyer to think the business is worth less. This conflict occurs almost every time a business is for sale. The true value of a business will always be what a ready, willing, and able buyer is willing to offer; and what the seller is willing to accept. This is the magical meeting of the minds and the true value of the business. Every other valuation, appraisal, or brokers opinion of value is just that – an opinion.

There are many reasons for conducting a business valuation. The most common are for the sale of the business to a third party, for litigation, for divorce, to buy out a partner, or to obtain special financing. You shouldn't be surprised if for each reason a different value is determined. In fact, the reason for determining the value of business may be the most important factor that goes into a valuation. Other factors include the value of tangible and intangible assets, risk factors, and the structure of the purchase.

Type of Assets Included in the Sale

First lets take a look at the type of assets that have value and can be transferred to a buyer. The two types of assets transferred in the sale of a business are *tangible assets* such as furniture, fixtures, and equipment (FF&E) and *intangible assets* such as intellectual property, trade secrets, and goodwill or "blue sky."

The tangible assets of a business include the furniture, fixtures, equipment, and vehicles that are used in the operations of the business. They may also include the inventory or the final goods that are to be sold. Whatever the tangible assets are they can be seen, touched, and physically measured. Most importantly they can be defined, and therefore, given a value that can then be sold, transferred, or assigned to somebody else.

Intangible assets are non-monetary in nature and cannot been seen, touched, or physically measured. They include such things as the brand recognition, proprietary processes, copyrights, patents, or trade secrets. By themselves, these intangible assets may have very little to no value. But as part of an ongoing business, they can be extremely valuable. They are such things as a "great name," "great customer service," or a "strong reputation" in the market.

Understanding Goodwill

The most common intangible asset is goodwill or "Blue Sky." Goodwill and is the difference between the fair market value of a

78

company's assets (less its liabilities) and the market price or asking price for the overall company. In other words, goodwill is the amount in excess of the company's book value that a purchaser would be willing to pay to acquire the company.

The wonderful thing about the value of an ongoing business is that the total value of the business is usually greater then the sum of the parts. Now before we get too far we need to understand that some business don't have any goodwill or blue sky. The value of these businesses may only be the value of a company's assets. Goodwill is probably the most intangible of all intangible assets. It is hard to measure and even more difficult to account for. It often becomes the focus of the negotiations between a buyer and seller and the biggest obstacle to achieving an offer and acceptance.

Business Valuation Process

There are at least nine different formulas or methodologies that we know of to value a business (there are probably a lot more that we don't know about). Each approach focuses on something different and may be applicable for different types of businesses. The three broad approaches are the Asset Approach, Income Approach, and Market Approach. The asset approach focuses on the tangible assets of the business and how much it would cost to replace those assets. The income approach focuses on the income generated by the business and future cash flow streams it generates. The market approach is based on the principal of substitution and therefore focuses on market data and comparable transactions.

Most business appraisers will use more then one formula to calculate a value. They will weight the results based on reasonable facts of the market, industry, and overall risk of the business to derive a blended business valuation.

Business brokers, on the other hand, will provide a Brokers Opinion of Value based on the Most Probable Selling price of the business. The methodology they follow is the Multiple of Seller's

Discretionary Earning or the Direct Market Data Approach. The steps they follow include the following:

1. Adjusting, or recasting, financial statements
2. Identifying the appropriate income multiplier
3. Determining the final business value

Adjusting or Recasting the Financial Statements

The first step in the business valuation process is to recast the financials statements. This means that balance sheet and the profit and loss statements are adjusted, or recast, to reflect a true and accurate picture of the business before the accountants step in and makes changes to reduce tax liability.

There are two reasons for preparing financial statements. The first is for managers to monitor the performance of the company. The second is for the Internal Revenue Service to know how much taxes are owed. So on one hand, managers are trying to increase net income and profits, and on the other hand accountants are trying to reduce taxes by driving net income down and as close as zero as possible. Recasting the financial statements brings the numbers back to a position that a buyer can analyze objectively.

Adjusted financial statements should paint a clear picture of the business's performance over a period of time – normally 3 to 5 years. The end result of the recasting exercise is a number called Seller's Discretionary Earnings or SDE. Other terms that are synonymous with SDE are Cash Flow, Adjusted Net Income, Profits, or Earnings. We hear it all the time, "How much cash flow does this business generate?" What they are really asking is how much SDE does this business generate.

The formula for calculating SDE is as follows:

Net Income
+ Interest Expense
+ Depreciation & Amortization
+ Owner Add Backs
= Sellers Discretionary Earnings

Interest expense is added back because potential buyers will have different financing arrangement then the current owner. Depreciation and amortization are added back because they are technically non-cash items for most businesses. Owner add-backs are those things that the business owner "runs through" their business but are not essential to the performance of the business. Things might include the owner's salary (since he will no longer be employed after the sale), life insurance for the owner, or cell phone use for the owner's children who work part time in the business.

Identifying the Appropriate Income Multiplier

The income multiplier is a factor (a number) times the Seller Discretionary Earnings that gives us the value of the business. How the income multiplier is identified is the tricky part of the business valuation process.

Because the Direct Market Data Method relies on the principle of substitution, it would make sense that a buyer would not pay any more for a business then that which they would have to pay for an equally desirable business. Looking at transactions that have closed in the past would give us an idea of what the business might bring as a sales price.

There are several sources that provide data on closed business sales, acquisitions, and mergers. These sources are available to anyone for a reasonable price. BizComps is the largest database for small business less than one million dollars in value. Pratts Stats is

81

the most reliable source for business worth more than one million dollars in value. The Institute of Business Appraiser (IBA) also has a large database of small to mid sized business transactions. A final source is a business broker – one that has been around long enough to capture data on closed transactions.

There are statistical rules that need to be followed in order to use this data appropriately. Analyzing the data and making accurate conclusion regarding the results takes years of experience to perfect. We recommend that you get a licensed business appraiser or trained business broker to assist you with this step in the process.

You may be tempted to use the "rule of thumb" in determining the value of a business. If that works, then every small business would sell for .44 times Gross Sales or 2.4 times SDE and every mid-sized business would sell for 6.7 times EBITDA. These are the factors resulting from the thousand of closed transactions in BizComps and Pratt Stats. Please don't make the mistake of using a rule of thumb to value your business. You will almost certainly price your business too high or too low and neither the buyer or the seller will benefit in the end.

The formula for calculating business value is as follows:

SDE x Income Multiplier = Business Value

Determining the Final Business Value

The final business value is a not complete without adding in specific assets and accounting for the fluctuation in working capital. Understanding what assets need to be added back to the business value is a matter of knowing what is included in the sale. The most common assets included in the sale of a business are the furniture, fixtures, equipment (FF&E), the vehicles, the inventory, and the real estate. The real estate may be sold as part of the transaction or leased back to the new owner.

The working capital (current assets minus current liabilities) will fluctuate between the time an offer is made and the deal is closed. Therefore, an adjustment is made either up or down to the selling price at the time of closing.

The most common and obvious adjustment is for inventory, but don't forget about the receivables and payables that may be included as part of the sale. At the time an offer is made the buyer expects there to be a certain amount of inventory included in the sale of the business. If the closing doesn't happen for 3 months, the amount of inventory is likely to either be more or less than at the time the offer was made. The difference between the asking price and the actual selling price is the working capital adjustment.

Chapter 5 – Selling Your Business

Every business is unique and no two business transactions are ever the same. To say that there are set steps in selling a business is a little bit of a misnomer. It is true there is a system and there are steps that can be followed sequentially. But not all business transactions follow the exact set of steps listed in this chapter. The following steps are derived from years of experience and describe the most typical steps in the selling process.

Step 1 – Make the Decision to Sell

We have already discussed this topic in earlier chapter of this book and you should be familiar with all the factors that need to be considered. You don't want to start the selling process unless you are willing to complete the task. There is too much work involved with the preparation, listing, and marketing of your business to not be 100% committed to selling the business. One of the worst strategies we see is the business owner that says, "I think I will just throw it out there and see what I can get for my business." You run some pretty serious risks with that type of approach including the loss of quality employees, vendors, and customers.

The process of selling isn't painless and it isn't quick. You need to make sure you want to sell before you begin. As a part of the decision making process it helps to know what you are going to do if you sell the business. You will have to spend awhile helping the new owner on a consulting basis but once that is complete you will have signed a non-compete and won't be able to compete in the industry or the area. Think about your exit strategy. If it is retirement, another business, travel, or just spending time with the family, make sure you have a plan.

Step 2 – Select the Right Business Broker

We have discussed the process of selecting the right business broker for your business type and size. The business broker will become an integral part of your business during the time you are selling your business. There certainly needs to be a level of trust between you and the broker. Both parties need to feel comfortable working together and strong channels of communication need to be established as the process unfolds and a deal comes together. Selecting the right business broker for your type of business and your personal style can make a difference between selling the business successfully or not.

Step 3 – Gather the Needed Information

Much of the information required to value, list, and market your business will be readily available to you if you have completed the Steps to Maximizing the Value of your Business. If not, don't worry, now is the time to get the information and be ready when it is needed. Below is a general list of what will be needed to sell your business.

- 3-Years of Financial Statements (Profit & Loss, Balance Sheet)
- Interim Financial Statements (Year To Date)
- 3-Years of Tax Returns
- Detailed List of Outstanding Debt
- List of Assets Included in the Sale
- Copy of Agreements and Contract
- Copy of Lease Agreement (Property and Equipment)
- List of Owner Perks and Benefits

One helpful hint is to make copies of the originals and only give the copies to the business broker or potential buyers. Even better is to provide the information in electronic format. The exchange of information is becoming increasingly digital and buyers are beginning to expect information electronically. You can easily scan documents and share them using email or the Internet.

As more buyers are introduced to your business, additional information will be required above and beyond what we have listed. This might include franchise agreements, contracts with vendors and customers, organizational charts, sample invoices, customer lists, etc. A good business broker will know how much information should be shared before an Offer to Purchase or Letter of Intent is required. If too much information is being requested without a formal offer in place, then the information should not be shared until an agreement on the purchase can be made.

Step 4 – Organize Yourself

The business broker will spend a significant amount of time marketing your business, interviewing and qualifying buyers, exchanging information, and negotiating terms and conditions. Unfortunately, they cannot do it alone. You should understand that the selling process will require your time and effort as well. You need to help collect all the information required, be available for answering questions about your business, and flexible in meeting potential buyers.

We suggest that you spend a little extra time organizing information and planning your calendar to accomplish selling your business.

Step 5 – Determine The Value of Your Business

We spent a whole chapter on determining the value of your business. Rather than go over the information just refer to that chapter. Keep in mind that this is really the responsibility of a business broker or licensed business appraiser. They should provide what is called a brokers opinion of value of the most probably selling price or a certified business appraisal respectively.

Once you have that information you can determine the asking price or the business.

Determining the right asking price is critical for attracting qualified buyers. List the asking price too high and you won't attract any buyers. List the asking price too low, and you may leave money on the table. One strategy is to list the asking price just slightly higher then the anticipated selling price knowing full well that the buyer will try and negotiate the price down. The buyer is satisfied when the price is reduced and the seller is satisfied knowing they received what they expected. Consultation with your business broker will help you understand where you should be listing the company.

Step 6 – Sign the Listing Agreement

Once you are ready to begin the process you will sign a representation or listing agreement with the business broker. Don't be afraid to ask questions about the agreement. Every business broker has a different agreement but they all contain essentially the same provisions. There is nothing to hide in the agreement and you should be assured that what you are signing is what you have agreed to in the process. Be sure to understand the term of the agreement and the price you will pay for services.

Step 7 – Prepare Your Story

As explained previously in another chapter of this book, your business story is an important component of the selling process. Give some thought and consideration to your sales pitch. Make a list of the selling points that would attract potential buyers and highlight the opportunity that exists.

You wouldn't walk into a sales call completely unprepared without any sales material to describe the product or service. Instead, you would be prepared with sales material, product descriptions, and service explanations at your fingertips, professionally prepared, and ready to present. There is nothing different in the selling process. People like to believe they are buying something special with a unique history and a compelling future. Your story should set you apart from the crowd and highlight the potential opportunity. They want to know that what they are purchasing a good opportunity, whether it is financial or just because the story and the history are so unique, and they want to be part of something different.

Step 8 – Assets to be Included in the Sale

The chart below is an example list of assets. You should have something similar that describes the assets to be included in the sale.

Description	Serial #	Cost	Market Value
HP LaserJet 4300	XNT4567	$350	$150
Roller Chairs Black		$79	$25
Ford F150	28392832	$21,500	$14,290
Racking System 290	TRZ890	$14,250	$11,970
	Total	$36,179	$26,435

Most small business sales in the U.S. are structured as assets sales and not stock sales. Therefore, any potential buyer is going to purchase the assets of your company and not its stock. They want to know what it is they are buying.

You would hate to see a deal come apart because the assets included in the sale weren't documented correctly. Unfortunately, we have seen this happen before. The buyer thought they were getting something different than what was actually be sold.

Another reason for accurately documenting the assets included in the sale for financing purposes. When a buyer wants to buy your business, they almost always (95% of the time) have to obtain some bank financing in order to make the purchase. When they go to the bank the underwriters want to know what assets are available to lend against for collateral.

Real estate is perhaps the most important assets included in the sale. Commercial lenders are more willing to take real estate as collateral then just about any other asset. The second most valuable asset is probably the equipment. With a complete and verifiable list of equipment the buyer can maximize the amount of money they can borrow from the bank. Having a current list will keep the ball rolling and allow the buyer to find out how much money the bank will lend for the acquisition.

Step 9 – Identify and Qualify Buyers

The time has now come to start looking for buyers who can acquire your business. This process involves two steps – first, identifying a pool of buyers that may have an interest in purchasing your business, and second is qualifying potential buyers based on their financial capacity and fit with the company.

In order to identify a pool of buyers you must share some information about the opportunity that exists. One of the most important documents a business broker will prepare is called a Blind Profile. This document contains generic information about your business, is usually less than a page, and provides the contact information of the broker. For confidentiality reasons, it does not include the names of the owners or any other information that would reveal the name of the company. The blind profile gives a general description of the business, its location and industry. It will also provide a summary of the financial performance – revenues, cash flow, and the value of the FF&E and inventory included in the sale – and the asking price for the business. The Blind Profile provides just enough information to get a buyer interested, but not enough information to reveal the identity of the company being sold.

A buyer who receives the blind profile information and expresses interest in the business will be required to sign a confidentiality agreement. The potential buyer should also demonstrate that they have the ability to acquire the business. This is accomplished a couple of ways. Our firm requires potential buyers to complete a buyer registration form as part of the confidentiality agreement. The information on the registration form is usually enough information to determine if the buyer is qualified or not. You may also request a personal financial statement, banker's reference, or a copy of their credit report. Once the buyer's registration form is returned and the confidentiality agreement has been executed, then the buyer will receive additional information to analyze the company.

There are numerous ways to identify potential buyers – traditional print advertising, radio and TV, direct mail campaigns, web-based multiple listing services, word of mouth, flyers and brochures, and from brokers representing buyers – just to name a few. The discussion that follows describes a couple of the most effective ways to attract buyers.

The Internet

Most business brokers will subscribe to a number of web-based multiple listing services on the Internet. The most popular sites include bizbuysell.com, bizquest.com, and businessesforsale.com. Today's business buyer will spend a significant amount of time searching the Internet for the right business to acquire and the best opportunities. The exchange of information on the Internet happens so quickly that buyers can literally be evaluating ten or twenty businesses at a time. A buyer can search by asking price, location, type of industry, profits generated, etc. They eventually zero in on the type of business and location they want.

On the other end of the Internet is the business broker facilitating the exchange of information with the buyers. The business broker generally has to spend a significant amount of time qualifying buyers in this process. Since the Internet casts a large web (pun intended) not all buyers are qualified and not all inquiries are legitimate. Regardless, the Internet is the primary source of buyer referrals and the number one method for attracting potential buyers.

Brokers Database of Buyers

All quality business brokerages keep an in-house list or database of buyers who are actively looking for businesses in their area of focus and have been provided information about their specific business requirements. These are buyers who have inquired regarding other business opportunities in the past and are interested in buying something that meets their needs. These buyers have made an effort to keep informed about the many business opportunities that exist and are willing to analyze each new listing that comes along.

Many business owners are surprised to learn that the typical individual buyer has no preconceived ideas about the type of business they want to own. With this being the case, many individuals are willing to look at just about any opportunity that makes sense. Many buyers (individuals. partnerships, and companies) are ready at a moments notice to consider most types of business opportunities. These buyers are pre-qualified and have the capacity to structure an acquisition and close the deal professionally and efficiently.

Targeted Buyers

A targeted buyer is one that may have a strategic reason – in addition to a financial reason – to acquire a business. A strategic buyer is usually another company in the same industry or a complementary industry. It may make sense for a company in one state seeking to expand market share into another state to purchase a similar company and grow their business through acquisitions. Another name for targeted buyers is strategic buyers because they have a strategic imperative compelling them to make acquisitions.

Targeted buyers may not be actively looking for an acquisition. However, a good business broker will be able to access the decision makers of the company and introduce the opportunity to them. A business broker has access to this kind of data and can identify the most likely strategic buyers and they will dedicate the time and resources necessary to contact these buyers.

Remember that you will want to set the terms and conditions for contacting these companies. If you don't want your local competitors to know you are for sale, you may tell the business broker to only search for out of state competitors or competitors that are at least 250 miles away. Consider what is best for you and have your business broker do the work.

Included in this category of buyers are Private Equity Groups or PEG's. These are investment companies looking to buy companies in specific industries to expand their portfolio and generate profits. Their model is to aggressively grow the company and then sell it five to seven years down the road for a much higher price. Most PEG's are looking for businesses that have at least one million dollars in EBITDA (Earnings Before Interest Taxes Depreciation and Amortization) and managers that can stay in place and run the company. PEG's are accountable to their investors and motivated by the bottom line return on the investment. If the deal doesn't pencil out, they will walk away not looking back for one second.

It is worth noting at this point that the average amount of time to sell a business is 9 months. Frequently it takes longer than that. It simply takes time to find the right buyer.

Step 10 – Maintain Confidentiality

With the business now on the market interested buyers will begin asking questions and requesting additional information. Before any information is giving to a buyer, they should have read, agreed to, and signed a buyers confidentiality agreement. Maintaining confidentiality becomes more important as the exchange of information takes place.

The worst thing you can do is give a buyer all the information they will ever need right up front. For one, it will be very overwhelming to them. Secondly, it is a waste of time and resources if they decide not to pursue the business any further. And finally, you don't want to give all that information to an unscrupulous buyer with insincere intentions that could possible damage your business. We prefer to give out additional information only as the buyer requests. This of course slows down the process. But in the end it is a better approach.

The language in a confidentiality agreement (a.k.a NDA or non-disclosure agreement) is meant to protect you and your business from a buyer disclosing critical information. This is especially important because the next step in the process is to give the buyer the business-offering memorandum describing the business in full detail. In order to understand the provisions of a confidentiality agreement, we included in the appendix of this book some of the most common language from these agreements.

Step 11 – Business Offering Memorandum

Now that the potential buyer has signed the confidentiality agreement and has proven to be a qualified buyer with the ability to purchase the company, he will be given the business offering memorandum. This memorandum is a report that describes the company, its ownership, management, customers, competition, products and services, and an analysis of the financial performance including financial statements. This report is normally prepared by the business broker and approved by the seller before it is offered to the buyers.

The business offering memorandum has several purposes including being a data sheet and a sales brochure. It also sets the standard for exchanging information and reinforces the need for confidentiality. A professionally prepared business offering memorandum is very important. It gives the buyer a first impression of the business, creates credibility and trust, and is helpful in analyzing the business opportunity. The memorandum sets the stage for additional questions and may persuade the buyer to further pursue the business.

The business offering memorandum should not include full financials, tax returns, or customer lists. This type of vital information should be held until the buyer has substantially confirmed their interest and pursued a set of questions and inquires. Just as a general practice you should not disclose your customer list until the buyer has made some type of offer or made an earnest money deposit.

Step 12 – Finding the Right Buyer

At this point a word needs to be said about the difference between finding a buyer and finding the right buyer – and there is a big difference. There are numerous buyers out there looking for businesses to buy. Most of them are tire kickers that will never successfully purchase a business. Then there are a few really good buyers that can close quickly, have the cash for a down payment, have the skills to run the business long term, the personality to work with your employees, and the capacity to honor the terms and conditions of the sale. The type of buyer you are looking for is the later of the two.

It is helpful to remember that only 2 out of every 100 buyers that inquire about a business will actually end up buying a business. You will go through a number of buyers to find the right buyer. Be patient and willing to work with each of the buyers in the process. Don't immediately discount any buyer until you have had an opportunity to evaluate the buyer and make a determination yourself. Sometimes first impressions are not the best impressions. Be willing to work with buyers until you know whether than can make it work long term. We have misjudged buyers before by jumping to conclusions too early in the process. Some of the best deals we put together have been with buyers that we wanted to discount after our first interactions with them. Luckily, they were persistent and eventually the deal happened.

Last suggestion on this topic is to be aware that a quality business broker will screen many of the buyers for you. Some brokers just want to sell your business to whoever will make an offer no matter the price or terms and conditions. If that is the case then you have the wrong broker. A quality business broker should find you the right buyer for the right price with the right terms and conditions.

Step 13 – Buyer and Seller Meeting

The buyer has received your information, signed a confidential agreement, gone through a list of questions with the business broker, analyzed your numbers, had a conference call with you and the business broker, and is now ready to visit the seller and tour the business. Orchestrating a successful onsite visit takes a little planning. You want the buyer to like what they see and recognize the business opportunity for what it is worth.

The business broker should conduct the tour of the business and allow you to answer questions and tell your story. Begin the onsite meeting by sitting down in the seller's office and doing a little relationship building. This is also a good time to share your story – how the business was started, how the products and services were developed, what challenges you overcame along the way, and the reason for selling the business. You may also want to share a little bit about you personally. Maybe something about your family or your hobbies – whatever seems appropriate to build a relationship of trust.

During this initial meeting the seller should be prepared to learn something about the buyer. We suggest that you try to learn as much about the person, or group, that intends to purchase you business as you can. Ask the buyer about his past business experience, educational background, or family situation. Try to determine why the buyer is motivated to buy the business and what goals they are trying to achieve. All of this information will be useful down the road when the structure of the deal is being defined. You will learn very quickly that both the needs of the buyer, as well as the seller, have to meet in order to successfully transfer business ownership.

Be prepared to walk around the facilities and show them how you do business. Hopefully the buyer has done some homework as well and is prepared to learn about the business. Individual buyers may be moving into an industry or a market that is new. Don't be surprised if they ask questions that are irrelevant or naïve. Take your time and show them all aspects of the business. Be willing to answer questions. The business broker will deflect any questions that may be inappropriate at this stage of the selling process. They may also interject with some questions that draw out some of the more positive aspects of the business. Once the tour is done be willing to sit again and answers questions that may not have been asked during the tour.

As we discussed earlier you need to decide how to handle your employees during the onsite visit. If you decide to conduct the onsite visit during business hours, your employees may wonder what is happening. Review the options we mentioned in prior chapters of this book for handling confidentiality issues.

Step 14 – Offer to Purchase the Business

Assuming the onsite visit went well and all other concerns have been resolved, the buyer should be ready to make an offer to purchase the business. We should point out that a buyer will always want more information. You can't blame them for wanting to feel comfortable about the decision to purchase your business. But there is no such thing as perfect information. Furthermore, it is impossible to eliminate all the risk associated with buying a business or establish one hundred percent confidence the buyer can be successful. At some point both parties just need to move forward. The best way to do this is with an Offer to Purchase or a Letter of Intent.

If you let the buyer run free asking for every last piece of information, you will eventually run out of patience and get frustrated. Don't get caught in that trap. At a certain point in the process the buyer needs to demonstrate that they are sincerely interested in purchasing the company. In fact, it is not good enough to just be sincere. They must prove they are willing to make a commitment and "put some skin in the game."

Prior to an offer being made don't allow the buyer to do extensive due-diligence such as accessing your customer list, contacting your vendors or employees, or reviewing bank accounts. You must first have a meeting of the minds and an offer in place before releasing that level of information.

In our firm we begin pushing the buyer to make an offer as soon as we can. Usually this is after the onsite visit when the momentum is strongest. The offer can be made in one of three ways:

Terms Sheet – Outlines the basic terms of conditions being offered by the buyer, usually less than a couple of pages long, non-binding, and used to see if the buyer and seller are close to a meeting of the minds.

Letter of Intent – Outlines the basic terms and conditions being offered by the buyer, usually more detailed with proposed timelines to close the deal, may included conditions to close (contingencies), is written in letter format, and is non-binding except for the obligation of both parties to proceed in good faith to close the deal. An example of a letter of intent is included in the appendix.

Offer to Purchase - Outlines the basic terms and conditions being offered by the buyer, attempts to cover most of the details associated with the transaction, includes the conditions to close, should include provisions for depositing earnest money, and is an enforceable binding agreement that compels both parties to honor the agreement.

Step 15 – Negotiations

There is always some degree of negotiations in selling your business. The buyer and the seller must negotiate so that both party's needs are satisfied. For a lot of people this is the worst part of the selling process. The good feelings that each party had prior to the negotiations can be shattered quickly in going back and forth on details that may seem small and unimportant at the time.

It has been said that you can either pick your price or your terms – but you can't pick both. We try to emphasize that terms and conditions are more important to a deal than price. Of course there are always exceptions. Don't get lost in the details or the intellectual and psychological warfare that may occur during this part of the process. If you can't step back and look at the big picture, then you are likely to loose a lot of sleep over nothing. At the same time, know your boundaries and be firm on those issues which will make a difference in the long run. It is better to have great terms and conditions on a transaction then to argue for that last $50,000 in a $1,500,000 transaction. Don't trip over a dollar to save a nickel. We will cover tips for negotiating in the next chapter.

Step 16 – Due Diligence

Once an offer has been made and accepted, then the buyer will begin the exercise of due diligence. This is the point where you are going to open up the company for the buyer to review the books and operations of the business to verify, validate, or prove that what you have represented to them is factual and accurate. Remember, you should not allow extensive due diligence to happen until the buyer has made an earnest money deposit and opened escrow. In a typical offer the earnest money deposit is refundable at any point during the due diligence period. After the initial period is over, then the escrow money becomes non-refundable to the buyer.

We have seen multi-million dollars companies purchased with less than one day of due-diligence and we have seen small businesses purchase only after weeks of due-diligence. It depends upon the buyer and the circumstances. It is likely that the buyer seller relationship will last long after the deal has closed. Remember to be helpful to the buyer during this process so you don't spoil that relationship.

An example due diligence checklist has been included in the appendix of this book.

Step 17 – Definitive Agreement

The most important document for legally and professionally transferring business ownership is the definitive agreement – also called the purchase and sale agreement or the asset purchase agreement. You should have your attorney draft this document and prepare it for the closing. Normally the seller's attorney drafts the agreement and the buyer's attorney reviews it; however, it can be done by either side. One approach is this; if the buyer has posted earnest money that is now non-refundable, have the seller's attorney draft the document. If the buyer hasn't posted earnest money, then request that the buyer's attorney to draft the document. This protect the seller from incurring unnecessary attorneys fee and get the buyer to throw a little more skin the game. The definitive agreement becomes the enforceable documentation in case a dispute arises after the transaction is closed.

The detail of the definitive agreement includes all the representation and warranties being made by both the seller and buyer. For the most part, this is just standard legal language that seems too wordy and too complicated for most peoples liking. However, we encourage you to understand the contents of the document and the promises being made by both parties and the consequences that may follow.

For larger transactions that contain multiple locations, real estate, more than a handful of employees, and several levels of complexity, then enlisting the services of a competent law firm is mandatory. For small transactions with less than a million dollars, just a handful of employees, leased facilities, and a simple business model, a boiler plate purchase and sale agreement my be all that is required.

A word about your attorney and your accountant seems appropriate at this point in our discussion. You contract with them to complete a certain task. No doubt you should listen to their advice and leverage their expertise. However, they should ultimately do what you direct them to do. We have seen too many attorneys and accountants kill deals for a variety of reasons – most of which are irrational and unfounded. Be sure your team of advisors are dealmakers and not deal killers. They are paid by the hour so the longer they work on this the more they are paid. They can have a tendency to make a mountain out of a small legal molehill. Don't let this happen. Listen to their advice, consider the options, make your decision and direct them how to proceed. Be careful not to let the bill run up and allow them to argue every tiny legal detail.

You will want your accountant to get involved early on in the process so you can structure a deal that limits your tax consequences. At a minimum your accountant should look the transaction over before you sign it so you will know the outcome of the tax consequence. They can be helpful in structuring the transaction to minimize the effect of taxes.

Step 18 – Closing the Transaction

At last the time has come to close the transaction. This step is includes signing the definitive agreement (i.e. Purchase and Sale Agreement) and depositing the funds to acquire the business with the closing agent or escrow company. The closing indicates that all contingencies have been satisfied, due diligence has been completed, and all other closing documents have been prepared and submitted to the closing agent. The buyer will have to post the money for the purchase in an escrow account at this point as evidence of ability to fund the transaction.

A closing agent or escrow company generally handles the closing. For smaller transactions you may be able to handle the closing and the transfer of ownership at the same time, especially if it isn't a complicated transaction. However for larger transaction with titled equipment, multiple leases, real estate, etc, the closing will happen in the offices of the closing agent and then the transfer of ownership will follow as the documents are recorded, funds are verified, obligations are paid, and leases and titles are transferred. Sometimes this takes just a couple of days; other times it may take weeks.

Often times the most difficult part of the closing is getting the funds from the commercial lender. The lender will have their own set of requirements and documents that will need to be included as part of the closing. It is not uncommon for the lender to get a little carried away with information required from the seller and buyer. You can't really blame them for trying to cover their basis and mitigate their risk. Regardless, it can be pretty frustrating for all the parties involved when the bank keeps requesting additional information or suggesting changes to the legal documentation.

Step 19 – Transfer of Ownership

The time has finally come to transfer ownership from the seller to buyer. An offer was made and accepted. Documents were prepared and signed. Money was deposited and funded. Titles were transferred and recorded. The seller has their money and the buyer has a new business to run. Now the real work begins.

There will be some tedious tasks that need to be completed after the sale. Things like changing over the utilities, phones, and contact information from the seller's name to the buyer's name. Most likely there will be a few dollars exchanged after the sale to makes things equal out. Once again, don't get hung up counting pennies. We suggest that you take the high road on these immaterial details in order to build goodwill, trust, and a strong relationship with the buyer as you move forward into the next phase of your life. If you absolutely must collect an extra thirty dollars from the buyer for paying a month in advance for the garbage to be collected, then go for it. But don't be surprised if the buyer starts to "nickel and dime" you right back.

The seller will most likely be expected to train the buyer for a certain amount of time – up to one year in some cases. This training period is extremely important to the future success of the business. If the seller financed a portion of the sale, then they have even more reason to stay close to the business and ensure the transition goes smoothly. This includes facilitating relationships with employees, vendors, landlords, and customers. There should be no reason for the business to skip one beat as the transition takes place.

We have observed several things that happen after the sale of the business. Sometimes the business will actually see a spike in sales as employees put forth a little more effort to impress the new owners. Vendors and customers seem to respond positively to the new owners as well. We believe this is because somebody (meaning the buyer) has validated that the business was valuable and purchased the right to be the owner. This seems to increase the confidence of these onlookers and encourages them to do more business. Other times there is a slight drop in sales as the new owner feels their way through the learning process. Be prepared for either outcome.

The final thing that we have observed is how quickly the buyer learns the business. Before the sale they think they need the seller to stick around and help run the business for an extended period of time. But quickly they realize that the seller is standing in their way and they want them gone as soon as possible. Often the old ideas of the seller hold the business back and the buyer wants to move on with their own way of doing things. Don't be surprised if the buyer kicks you out the door sooner than you expected.

Chapter 6 – Negotiating the Deal

Negotiating the deal is a major step in the selling process and since it will greatly affect the outcome, we felt it appropriate to spend sometime providing additional information on the nuances of the negotiating process. We have provided some of our tips and tricks for negotiating a successful deal.

Appeal to a higher authority – One of the universal tactics in negotiations is to make the other party believe the final decision doesn't rest with you. This is very difficult to accomplish if the party doing the negotiating is also the party responsible for the final decision. As a business broker and intermediary we can always say, "I have to check with my client to see if that will be acceptable or not." This postpones the decision and relieves the pressure that might otherwise result in a bad decision. Plus it puts the buyer in the position of not wanting to appear cheap or insulting.

Get it in writing – Thinking out loud regarding the structure of a deal can have devastating consequences. We have seen it happen all to often where the seller throws out a number (i.e. asking price, carry back, etc.) and the buyer never forgets it and, even worse, holds them to it throughout the negotiating process. Rather then think out load, use something simple like a terms sheet to facilitate the back and forth of the terms and conditions.

Don't chase the buyer – Acting too interested in the buyers offer appears like you are desperate to sell and basically eliminates any negotiating position that you might leverage. This is especially obvious when the business owner (seller) continues to initiate the discussion with the buyer. However, having a business broker constantly following up on the buyer appears quite normal because that is their job.

Have more than one offer – The only thing better than a good offer is two good offers. Buyers don't particularly enjoy the bidding war and most will try to avoid it if they can. However, the seller that has two offers stacked side by side can easily pick and choose those terms and conditions that they like the most. If the buyers want the business bad enough, you can leverage these points to your advantage. Keep in mind that a buyer that feels manipulated will probably walk from the deal. So you must use this tactic carefully.

Be prepared to walk away – Just about everybody has heard this tip. It is the most effective negotiating tactic we know. However, if you walk away from a deal and later decide that you were wrong, the chances of going back to the table a very slim. If you have an intermediary doing the negotiations, then the "walk away" tactic is really a natural result of breaking off communications with that buyer. There is always an easy way for the broker to bring the deal back to the table.

It is kind of nice to have an intermediary handle the negotiations on your behalf. You can just sit back with no pressure and watch the process unfold. You must of course give your input and help the broker understand what you want to get from the deal. There have been times when the back and forth of the negotiations was either taking too long or was just simply not effective. Only in extreme cases should the buyer and seller get together and hash out the agreement. We have seen on occasion where the buyer and seller were able to sit down in a room and strike a deal. In this scenario the relationship of trust and goodwill had been established through months of interaction and both parties were determined to create a win/win situation. But under normal circumstances we recommend you enlist the help of a third party negotiator, business broker, or intermediary to help facilitate the negotiations.

Negotiating Levers

When the buyer and seller come together to strike a deal they come with the intentions to maximize their own self-interest or that of the stakeholders. They naturally want what is best for them and their particular situation. Rarely do both parties get exactly what they want. Successful transactions are ones where both parties make some concessions to help the other party and vice versa. If either the buyer or seller is unwilling to move from their position by drawing a hard line, the deal will almost always fall apart.

What you need to do is identify the negotiating levers that can be used to bring a deal together. Some of those levers are obvious, such as the price or seller financing provided. Others are less obvious bust just as effective. And finally, there are some negotiating levers that should be avoided if possible. Below is a list of the most common negotiating levers.

- Price vs. Terms
- Asset Sale vs. Stock Sale
- Purchase Price Allocation
- Consulting Agreements
- Non-Compete
- Earnest Money Deposit

Price vs. Terms

You have heard it said many times that you can pick your price or your terms, but you cannot pick both. Now there is always a person that says they sold their business for exactly the price and the terms that they wanted. If that is the true, then we have never met that person.

Most successful business transactions involve some amount of give and take and concessions are made to meet the needs of both parties. It is much more of a process that unfolds over time as the buyer and seller interact with each other and learn about their specific goals, dreams, and motivations. If one party is too demanding, the deal is sure to fall apart. We are certainly not suggesting that you just roll over and give in to every request. You must know your boundaries and determine realistic limits.

The price is the most obvious negotiating lever. There is significant amount of time spent by the seller, buyer, and broker analyzing numbers and determining what the final price should be. What is sometimes missed is this analysis is the fact that a lower price with favorably terms and conditions will most likely lead to more money in the seller's pocket when all is said and done. That is because the favorable terms, over time, will increase the total consideration (all monies, not just price) going to the seller.

The most common terms to be negotiated include the amount of cash at closing (buyers down payment), the amount of seller financing, any type of earn out, and the rate and term for a lease on the property if applicable.

Cash at Closing

Cash at closing becomes the first hurdle that both parties must overcome. The seller needs enough money at closing to pay off their liabilities, obligations, and debts. Remember that the assets of the business must pass free and clear of all liens and encumbrances to the buyer. That means that the seller must payoff any creditors before the deal can close. The seller must also pay closing cost such as the brokers commission, legal fees, transfer fees, title insurance (if real estate is included), and legal fees. The remaining money goes to the sellers as the proceeds from the sale.

The buyer down payment is the amount of money the buyer is investing in the business. Sometimes this is the person's life savings. We advise our clients to focus on the total consideration or amount of money that you will gain from the deal and not the actual purchase price.

Simply put you want the most cash up front as possible. You want the smallest amount of seller carry-back. You want the shortest term on the carry back and you want a market rate or higher on the interest rate. Be careful when agreeing to interest only terms, you never reduce the principal and it is hard for the buyer to pay that lump sum. Also if possible have the debt you carry back be termed out in full. Don't agree to a balloon payment. Keep in mind that this is the ideal situation and there should be give and take to arrive at a fair transaction, but the items listed above are critical to your success.

Seller Financing

Only 5% of all transactions are for all cash. Typically, all cash transactions are for businesses that sell for less than $100,000. Almost all businesses that sell for larger amounts will require the seller to finance a portion of the transaction. If the buyer is using the SBA to finance a portion of the deal, then the seller will be required to carry back a portion of the sales.

It is very typical for the seller to carry some portion of the sales price for a period of time. The question comes, how long, how much, and at what price. Before we cover those topics, remember, it isn't all bad being the bank. Here are some of the advantages to seller financing:

- You are going to collect an installment payment that may have some tax advantages
- You will be collecting an interest rate that will increase the total dollars you generate from the sale

- You will have security on the loan from the business assets and a personal guarantee from the buyer

There is really no set amount when it comes to how much seller financing to provide. In the past it was common to see the seller provide at least 25% of the financing. Just recently it has become more common for sellers to provide all of the financing and leave the bank out of the deal all together. As for the terms, it is better to get a principal and interest payment on a monthly or quarterly basis then one large balloon payments at the end of a term. Most carry-backs will involve a market or slightly higher than market rate of interest. We think it is too risky to tie the payback of the seller financing to some type of earn-out. A simple promissory note with a principal and interest payment amortized over a term of 3, 7, or 10 years is best.

The on-going success of the new buyer and your chances of getting paid in the future are key to negotiating smart terms and conditions. We always tell our clients that, "earn-outs never work out." An Earn Out is a way for the buyer to pay the seller based on the future performance of the business. There is no guarantee that the seller will ever get this money. Earn-outs are different than seller financing or seller carry-back – both of these arrangements are guaranteed payments secured by collateral.

Most earn outs are based on a certain level of earnings such as sales, gross profits, or net income. The difficulty comes when the buyer is now in charge of the income statement and has complete control over the operations of the company. Ultimately they can manipulate the numbers to their benefit and reduce the amount of money earned by the seller. It is a scenario where the fox is guarding the hen house. That is why we recommend avoiding earn-outs for most small business transactions.

In larger mid-market transaction an earn out may be acceptable. In these transactions you can find a level of income that is difficult to manipulate for the buyer, thus decreasing the risk of the new owners playing with the numbers. There may also be some kind of stock that is included in the earn out that will benefit the sellers total gain when all is said and done. Whatever the earn out is based on needs to be measured carefully to ensure that the seller gets a fair deal.

Consulting Agreements

Almost in every case you are going to be asked to stay on after the sale of the company to transfer your business knowledge, systems, relationships, and contacts to the new owner. It is a rare case that a seller just gets to walk away the next day. Your on-going consulting agreement could be as short at two weeks or as long as a year or two in some cases.

If you have financed a portion of the sales price, then it is in your best interest to make sure the transition is as smooth and seamless as possible. The buyer's success becomes your best chance for completely profiting in the deal. This transition process will take your time and effort. So don't plan on running away to some tropical island the day the deal closes. You will have to accept the fact that somebody else now owns the company and his direction is what you are trying to help achieve. Stepping down from the general's position to a lieutenant can be a challenge.

The good news is that you should be paid for this work. Since you don't own the company and yet you are still expected to work at the company, you should expect to be paid. There are many options for how you should be compensated for your work. You can work for an hourly rate and bill your time. You can work for a minimum number of hours a week for a flat fee. Or you can work for a flat salary with a list of tasks to be accomplished. Whatever the arrangement make sure it is clearly listed in the documentation. It should include your new job description, the number of hours you are required to work, and the amount of money you will be paid for you services.

Non-Compete Agreements

No buyer wants to buy your company only to have you immediately turn around and start competing for the same business. Therefore, you will be asked to sign a non-compete that will be for a specific period of time and generally a specific geographic area. In some cases it can specify certain product lines and services and allow you the freedom to pursue products and services that the new owner isn't interested in pursuing. Read the non-compete and make sure you understand the provisions. You should insure in the negotiations that if the buyer defaults on their obligations the non-compete is no longer enforceable. That will allow you the freedom to come back and quickly work the business in the event the buyer defaults and you have to take the business back (which, by the way, doesn't happen too often).

The caution here is if you intend to use the proceeds of the sale to pursue a business interest, then make sure it is not a conflict of interest and you have the right and power to pursue that business.

Earnest Money

Earnest money is a negotiating point. How much, when it is posted, when it becomes hard or non-refundable, and how it applies to the purchase price are all considerations. There is no set rule on the amount of earnest money. It should be significant enough to cause both parties to move ahead in closing a deal. An escrow company or some other type of trustee that can legally hold this type of money should always handle it. Attorneys and brokers normally have trust accounts for the purpose of holding earnest money deposits. As a seller you should make sure that somewhere during this process the earnest money goes hard or non-refundable. This event further commits the buyer and solidifies the deal. In some cases there may be scaled amounts that are non-refundable and certain time markers in the process. We have seen earnest money be 3% of the purchase price and other times 10% of the purchase price. In almost all cases the earnest money will applied towards the purchase price at the time of closing.

Most states frown on sellers who keep the buyers earnest money deposit without concrete evidence that the seller or his/her business was damaged in some way. Earnest money should not be viewed as punitive damages received for a deal that fails to close. We have seen on occasion provisions in a contract that specifies liquidated damages for which the earnest money could be applied. This is rare to such a provision in a business sales contract. Be sure to consult your legal advisor regarding this topic.

Purchase Price Allocation

The purchase price allocation assigns a value to all of the assets (tangible and intangible) being sold. It becomes a significant negotiating point because of the taxes consequences that will follow. The tax allocation is only applicable when it comes to an asset sale. This is an issue for your accountant to address and you should seek their help through the process.

From the seller's perspective, taxes will have to be paid on the gain of the sold assets. Normally, the tangible assets of the business have been fully depreciated so there is no gain.

From the buyer's perspective, the assets will be booked at the price stated in the purchase price allocation. This becomes the tax basis for those assets and the depreciation will be calculated from there. Depreciation is a non-cash item that ultimately reduces the amount a taxes that have to be paid by the buyer. The bottom for the buyer is that they want the ability to depreciate as much as possible going forward.

For example, suppose the purchase price allocation assigns $500,000 in equipment assets and $500,000 in blue sky or goodwill. The buyer can depreciate $500,000 in equipment assets immediately after the sale at that accelerated rate. This depreciation reduces the net income number and taxes that need to be paid. On the other hand, the blue sky or good will has to be depreciated over a much longer period of time. So the buyer will want to allocate almost all of the cost of the purchase to equipment assets and very little to the blue sky.

The seller generally speaking will want the reverse. They want very little allocated to the already depreciated equipment assets because everything above the depreciated tax book value will be taxed at an ordinary income rate. Without getting into the real specifics, just know that the buyer and seller are at odds on this issue. There are guidelines for the tax code but they can loosely interpreted.

The point to remember here is that you will want to involve your CPA in this process. Your CPA can tell you exactly what your tax consequence will be given the different allocation options. You will have to be flexible and workable in the process, but be aware that in negotiating you shouldn't allow the buyer to determine tax allocation. It should be a mutually agreeable result.

Stock sale vs. Asset sale

This really isn't a negotiating point. It should be determined before the company is listed. The company will be sold as either an asset sale or a stock sale. As mentioned earlier most of the time it is an assets sale. However, there is cause for a consideration of a stock sale. It really becomes an issue of half a dozen of one or 6's of the other. If you do an asset sale you can generally ask a higher price (but you will have a higher tax consequence) and if you do a stock sale you will likely get less for the company (but you will have a smaller tax consequence). Your business broker will help you with the valuations and the understanding of this process. The offset is simply the amount of taxes you will pay.

The liability a buyer will assume when they purchase your stock is another factor that will be considered. Once they own the company, they own the liability for past mistakes that may come back to haunt them. Because of this issue there is generally a discounted factor for the price. Take time to discuss the issues with your business broker and determine a valuation that is realistic based upon the type of sale you will pursue.

Working with the CPA and Attorney

This deserves some attention as a negotiating tool. The decision of who you work with when it comes to CPA's and an attorney is critical. They can play a major role in the process either for the good or for the bad. The number of deals that crash land because an attorney or a CPA is surprising. We know for a fact that 50% of all deals will fail to close. With such poor odds you need to make sure both your accountant and lawyer are dealmakers and not deal killers.

When it comes time to fully involve your accountant and attorney the majority of the terms have been agreed upon. You need their input and counsel to work through the details of the deal. Unfortunately, we have seen it happen more then once where they begin to question the buyer's motivation, posture to impress the client, attempt to re-negotiate terms, and overall complicate the deal. In the end you find that you don't have a deal at all.

On the flip side, you accountant and attorney can make your life wonderful by finding ways to make the deal sweater for both sides of the transaction. You need a problem solver not a problem finder. You should be working with advisors that are focused on a good deal and not just more billable hours. Your business broker should be able to give you some quality recommendation on who to use and what to expect with the process.

Conclusion

You should by now understand the process of selling a business. You should have a good sense of those factors that need to be considered before deciding to sell. And you should be comfortable with idea of working with professional advisors to successfully transfer business ownership. Hopefully we have planted in your mind some ideas that will make you more prepared for this exciting time in your life. You should commit some time to draft your own personal plan for maximizing business value while increasing personal wealth.

Don't forget that no two transactions are the same. Each set of circumstances is different and thus each business sale is different. There is no need to be afraid of the process and certainly, after reading this book, you will have a better understanding of what lies is ahead.

Obviously there is some preparation involved and that preparation will help you maximize the value of the company. Evaluate your circumstances and determine if now is the time to sell or if you have time to implement many of the items we have discussed. It may be that now is the time to sell and your preparation will stand on its own.

As the authors of this book we are committed to quality, ethics, and client satisfaction. It is for that reason that we are happy to include our contact information. We would be happy to answer any questions you may have and assist you in anyway for the smooth, profitable, and timely sale of your company.

Kelly Shaw
Business Broker
Kelly@BristolGroupOnline.com

Trevin Rasmussen, CBI
Business Broker
Trevin@BristolGroupOnline.com

Trevin Rasmussen
Office: 208-319-3800
Email: trevin@BristolGroupOnline.com
Address: 950 Bannock Street, Suite 1100, Boise, Idaho 83616

Trevin Rasmussen is an experienced main street and mid-market business broker. He is a Certified Business Intermediary (CBI) and an active member of the International Business Brokers Association (IBBA.org).

Prior to becoming a business broker he worked as a management consultant for Andersen Consulting (Accenture) and Arthur Andersen. Mr. Rasmussen has consulted Fortune 500 and mid-market companies in San Francisco, Seattle, and Boise. He has worked in several disciplines of business including finance, strategy, and technology.

Mr. Rasmussen is a member of the International Business Brokers Association, Boise Young Professionals, and Director of the Boise Chapter of the Management Society. He has a Master of Information Systems Management degree and a BS in Business Management from Brigham Young University.

Kelly D. Shaw

Office: 208-319-3800
Email: kelly@BristolGroupOnline.com
Address: 950 Bannock Street, Suite 1100, Boise, Idaho 83616

Kelly has been a partner in an investment banking and business consulting firm, an owner or manager of 15 privately held companies, and the founder of a distribution company that was acquired by a Cintas, a Fortune 500 Company. The combined operations included more than 200 employees and $25 Million in revenues.

He started his career nearly 30 years ago as a commercial loan officer in the banking industry. There he financed business start-ups, operations, and on-going cash needs for businesses.

Mr. Shaw is a member of the International Business Brokers Association. He is the author of two books, the director of a leadership camp, and father of 5 children. He holds a BA in International Relations with an emphasis on International Business from Brigham Young University.

Appendix

Listing Agreement

The following is provided as an example of an EXCLUSIVE LISTING AGREEMENT

The undersigned Seller hereby GRANTS to the undersigned Broker the EXCLUSIVE RIGHT TO SELL and authority to act as agent for a primary period of TWELVE (12) months from the date this Agreement is signed by the Seller to sell the business assets of the business known as _____, located at _____ ("Business").

PURCHASE PRICE:

The purchase price will be: $ _____(dollars), at such terms acceptable to the Seller.

TERMS OF SALE:

The business assets include the following (if initialed by Seller):

[___] [___] All the furniture, fixtures, equipment, leasehold improvements, and other tangible assets on the premises, with the following exceptions:
_____

[___] [___] All the trade, goodwill, and other intangible assets of the Business

[___] [___] All the inventory of the Business at the Sellers cost adjusted at the time of closing: $_____

[___] [___] All of the accounts receivable of the Business adjusted at the time of closing: $_____

[___] [___] Other _____

NOTICE: The amount or rate of the Brokers commission is not fixed by law. They are set by each Broker individually.

COMPENSATION TO BROKER. Seller agrees to pay Broker as compensation for services rendered a commission based on the terms and conditions and selling price as follows:

_____ percent of the first $1,000,000 of the sales price

_____ percent of the second $1,000,000 of the sales price

_____percent of the third $1,000,000 of the sales price

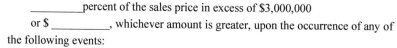

_____percent of the sales price in excess of $3,000,000

or $_____, whichever amount is greater, upon the occurrence of any of the following events:

The Broker produces a Buyer who offers to purchase the Business during the primary period above, or extension, on the terms specified above or any other terms acceptable by the Seller.

The Business is sold, exchanged, or otherwise transferred during the primary period above, or extension, by the Seller or through any other source.

Seller fails or refuses to complete a sale or any form of transfer of all or any part of the Business after entering into a written agreement with a Buyer.

Seller violates the terms of this Agreement and/or breaches any material warranty or representation made herein, or withdraws the Business from the market and/or otherwise attempts to terminate this agreement.

RETAINER. Broker shall be paid, upon execution of this Agreement, a retainer of_____. Such retainer shall be non-refundable, but shall be fully deductible from the commission due to Broker at any future closing within the term of this Agreement.

SELLER'S OBILGATIONS AND WARRANTIES.

Seller agrees to make available to Broker and prospective buyers all data, records, and documents pertaining to the business.

Seller agrees to allow Broker and cooperating brokers to show the Business at reasonable times and upon reasonable notice.

Seller agrees not to obstruct the Broker's performance in any way.

In the event of a sale, Seller will promptly deposit in escrow all instruments necessary to complete the sale.

In the event of a sale, Seller agrees to and does hereby irrevocably assign to Broker, compensation as provided above from the Seller's proceeds at closing.

Seller warrants the accuracy of the information provided with respect to the Business and agrees to hold the Broker harmless from any liability or damage arising out of incorrect or undisclosed information.

Seller warrants that he or she is the owner of record of the Business or has written authority to execute this Agreement on behalf of the owner(s) of record.

Seller warrants that he or she has not entered into any other listing agreement in force granting an exclusive agency to another broker.

In the event that Seller did not provide a retainer fee as noted above, Seller will be responsible for costs associated with appraising the business (if required), legal, accounting, and customary closing fees.

In the event that Seller did provide a retainer fee as noted above, Broker will pay for appraising the business (if required) and Seller will be responsible for the costs associated with legal, account and customary closing fees.

PROTECTION PERIOD. If the Seller effects the sale of a Related Business during the existence of this Agreement or within TWELVE (12) months after the termination of this Agreement and such sale is made to any Buyer or prospective Buyer with whom Broker or any cooperating broker had any contact regarding the sale of the Business during the existence of this Agreement, Broker shall be entitled to the compensation listed above.

AGENCY. Broker will use best efforts to represent Seller as its exclusive agent with EXCLUSIVE RIGHT TO SELL the Business until this Agreement is terminated. Seller acknowledges that Broker has not guaranteed the sale of the above Business. Broker is authorized to cooperate with other brokers in the marketing and sale or exchange of the Business and may divide the above compensation with the other brokers in any manner acceptable to them. It is understood that Broker is acting as agent for the Seller.

CONSENT TO LIMITED DUAL REPRESENTATION AND ASSIGNED AGENCY:

[___] [___] The undersigned have received, read and understand the Agency Disclosure Brochure.

SELLER NOTIFICATION AND CONSENT TO RELEASE FROM CONFLICTING AGENCY DUTIES: SELLER acknowledges the undersigned Broker has disclosed the fact that at times Broker acts as agent for other Sellers and for Buyers in the purchase of property. SELLER has been advised and understands that it could create a conflict of interest for Broker to introduce any CLIENT BUYERS to SELLER'S property because Broker could not satisfy all duties to both the Client Buyer and the Client Seller in connection with such a showing or any transaction which resulted.

Based on the understanding acknowledged, Seller makes the following election: (make one selection only)

[___] [___] Limited Dual Representation

Seller DOES WANT broker to introduce any interested client of the Broker to Client Seller's property and hereby agrees to relieve Broker of conflicting duties including the duty to disclose confidential information known to the Broker at the time and the duty of loyalty to either party. Relieved of all conflicting agency duties, Broker will act in an unbiased manner to assist the Buyer and Seller in the introduction of Buyer to such Client Seller's property and in the preparation of any contract of sale which may result. It is agreed that the Seller shall be notified by Broker whenever a Buyer Client of the Broker desires to see Seller's property

[___] [___] Single Agency

Seller DOES NOT WANT Broker to introduce interested Buyer Clients to Client Seller's property and hereby releases Broker from any responsibility or duty

125

under the agency agreement to do so. Broker shall be under no obligation or duty to introduce Buyer to any Client Seller's property.

BUSINESS EVALUATION. In no event shall Broker be required to participate in any evaluation of the Business, including, without limitation, any accounting, inventory, appraisal, audit, verification or other similar evaluation either for Seller or for a prospective buyer, and Seller hereby expressly releases and discharges Broker from any responsibility or liability in connection with any such evaluation. Seller hereby accepts sole and final responsibility for the evaluation of the Business. Further, Seller hereby expressly releases and discharges Broker from any responsibility or liability in connection with the integrity, creditworthiness, or actions of any prospective buyer or buyer of the Business.

INTERNET MARKETING AND POST-CLOSING DATA REPORTING. It is understood that the Broker has the right to share data about the business, or from any subsequent sale, lease or any other transaction hereunder, with any information-sharing databases with which Broker may have a cooperating agreement. This data may be shared, either for purposes of marketing the business for sale during the listing term, or for reporting the sale price and terms to a database after closing. Broker shall endeavor to camouflage the business identity if the Seller requests this, but cannot be held accountable for accidental breach of confidentiality from such post-closing networking or data reporting.

NON COMPETE. In connection with the sale of the Business, the Seller, at the request of buyer, may be asked to execute a Covenant Not To Compete in a form reasonably acceptable to buyer.

ARBITRATION OF DISPUTES. Any controversy between the parties to this Agreement involving the construction or application of any of the terms, covenants or conditions of this Agreement, shall on written request of one (1) party served on the other, be submitted to binding arbitration. Such arbitration shall be under the rules of the American Arbitration Association. The arbitrator shall have no authority to change any provisions of this agreement; the arbitrator's sole authority shall be to interpret or apply the provisions of this Agreement. The expenses of arbitration conducted pursuant to this paragraph shall be born by the parties in such proportion, as the Arbitrators shall decide.

ATTORNEY FEES. In any action, arbitration, or other proceedings to recover compensation as provided in this Agreement, the prevailing party will be entitled to recover reasonable attorney fees, expert witness fees, and costs to be determined by the court or arbitrator(s).

ENTIRE AGREEMENT. This document contains the entire agreement of the parties and supersedes all prior agreements with respect to the property which are not expressly set forth. All modifications must be in writing signed and dated by both parties.

LIMITATION OF AGENCY. Real estate brokers, business brokers, and agents are not qualified to give legal, tax, accounting, or insurance advice. For these questions, you should consult with your attorney, accountant, or insurance agent.

SPECIAL CONDITIONS. _____

_____

_____

_____

Buyers Confidentiality Agreement

Language of a Buyer's Confidentiality Agreement

"The Information is of a proprietary and confidential nature, the disclosure of which to any other party will result in damage to the Seller and/or Business, and Buyer further represents and warrants as follows:

(A) The Information furnished by Broker or Seller has not been publicly disclosed, has not been made available to Buyer by any party or source other than Broker or Seller and is being furnished only upon the terms and conditions contained in this Agreement.

(B) Buyer will not disclose the Information, in whole or in part, to any party other than persons within Buyer's organization, including independent advisers/consultants, who have a need to know such Information for purposes of evaluating or structuring the possible purchase of the Business. Buyer accepts full responsibility for full compliance with all provisions of this Agreement by such other persons.

(C) Buyer will not disclose, except to the extent required by law, to any parties other than the persons described in Paragraph 2(B) above that the Business is available for purchase or that evaluations, discussions or negotiations are taking place concerning a possible purchase.

(D) Buyer will not utilize, now or at any time in the future, any trade secret(s), as that term may be defined under statutory or common law, that is/are included in the furnished Information for any purpose other than evaluating the possible purchase of the Business, including, without limitation, not utilizing same in the conduct of Buyer's or any other party's present or future business(es).

(E) In addition to the prohibition against utilizing trade secret(s), Buyer will not utilize any other furnished information for any purpose other than evaluating the possible purchase of the Business, specifically including, without limitation, not utilizing same to enter into and/or engage in competition with the Business or assist or promote any other party(s) in so doing. The foregoing prohibition against utilizing said Information in competing with the Business shall remain in effect for three (3) years from the date hereof and shall be applicable to competition within the presently existing marketing area of the Business.

(F) If Buyer decides not to pursue the possible purchase of the Business, Buyer will promptly return to Broker all Information previously furnished by

Broker or Seller, including any and all reproductions of same, and further, shall destroy any and all analyses, compilations or other material that incorporates any part of said Information."

Buyer will not contact the Seller or Seller's employees, customers, suppliers or agents other than Broker for any reason whatsoever without the prior consent of the Broker. All contacts with the Seller or such other parties will be made through or by Broker unless otherwise agreed to by Broker, in writing.

Letter of Intent

Dear Mr. Smith,

The purpose of this letter is to set forth in outline form the mutual intent to negotiate and enter into an agreement (the "Definitive Agreement") whereby TED BUYER or his agents or assigns ("Buyer") will purchase the assets and certain liabilities of ONE GREAT BUSINESS, INC. owned by JIM SELLER ("Seller").

The proposed terms and conditions of this Letter of Intent include, but are not limited to the following:

A. Buyer will purchase the assets and liabilities of Seller as listed in Appendix A attached to this Letter of Intent in exchange for $ 4,500,000 (Purchase Price). The Buyer will deliver to the Seller on the Closing Date cash of $3,00,000. The Seller will loan the Buyer $1,500,000 and the Buyer will pay back the loan in monthly payments (principle and interest) for 10 years at an agreed upon interest rate. The Buyer will start making monthly payments six (6) months after the closing date.

B. The purchase price will be adjusted up or down at closing by the difference between the amount of inventory as of JUNE 1, 2009 and the amounts of inventory as of the Closing Date.

C. Buyer shall have thirty (30) days from the date that both Seller and Buyer sign this Letter of Intent to examine all records, conduct all investigations and perform all due diligence regarding this transaction.

D. Seller will provide a draft of a Definitive Agreement to Buyer incorporating the terms outlined herein and all other reasonable terms sixty (60) days from the date this Letter of Intent is signed by both Seller and Buyer.

E. The closing date for this transaction shall be on or before ninety (90) days from the date that both Seller and Buyer sign this Letter of Intent.

F. Seller will agree not to engage in any material financial transaction not in the ordinary course of business for a period not exceeding sixty (60) days from the date this letter is signed by both Seller and Buyer unless either party sooner terminates negotiation of this transaction.

G. All legal fees and other expenses on behalf of either party in connection with the transaction will be borne by the party incurring such expense.

H. Except for the provisions of Sections F and G above, this Letter of Intent shall not be binding on the parties and shall expressly be subject to the execution and approval of a Definitive Agreement by Seller and Buyer.

I. Seller will agree to train the Buyer for a period of 6 months after the closing date at a cost of $ 20,000 paid in one lump sum at the end of the training period.

J.   This Letter of Intent shall expire ninety (90) days from the date both Seller and Buyer have signed this Letter of Intent, unless, 1) Seller or Buyer sooner terminate negotiations in writing or, 2) Seller and Buyer mutually agree in writing to extend the term of the Letter of Intent, or 3) Seller and Buyer close the transaction.

K.   This letter of Intent may be executed in counterparts and may be delivered by facsimile transmission. Each such counterpart shall constitute an original, but all such counterparts shall constitute but one Letter of Intent.

L.   The word "days" means calendar days unless otherwise indicated.

This Letter of Intent is not a binding contract but does establish the obligation of the parties to proceed in good faith toward the preparation of the Definitive Agreement.

Due Diligence Checklist

1) Organization and Good Standing.
   a) The Company's Organizational papers.
   b) The Company's list of shareholders and number of shares held by each.
   c) A Certificate of Good Standing from the Secretary of State of the state where the Company is incorporated.

2) Financial Information.
   a) Financial statements for three years..
   b) The Company's credit report, if available.
   c) A schedule of all indebtedness and contingent liabilities.
   d) A schedule of inventory.
   e) A schedule of accounts receivable.
   f) A schedule of accounts payable.
   g) Tax Returns for the last three years.

3) Physical Assets.
   a) A schedule of fixed assets.
   b) All leases of equipment.

4) Real Estate.
   a) A schedule of the Company's business locations.
   b) Copies of all real estate leases, deeds, mortgages, title policies, surveys, zoning approvals, variances or use permits.

5) Employees and Employee Benefits.
   a) A list of employees including positions, current salaries, salaries and bonuses paid during last three years, and years of service.
   b) All employment, consulting, nondisclosure, non-solicitation or non-competition agreements between the Company and any of its employees.
   c) Résumés of key employees.
   d) The Company's personnel handbook and a schedule of all employee benefits and holiday, vacation, and sick leave policies.
   e) A list and description of benefits of all employee health and welfare insurance policies or self-funded arrangements.
   f) A description of worker's compensation claim history.
   g) A description of unemployment insurance claims history.

6) Licenses and Permits.

a)   Copies of any governmental licenses, permits or consents..

7)   Environmental Issues.
   a)   Environmental audits, if any, for each property leased by the Company.
   b)   A listing of hazardous substances used in the Company's operations.
   c)   A description of the Company's disposal methods.
   d)   A list of environmental permits and licenses.

8)   Customer Information.
   a)   A schedule of the Company's twelve largest customers in terms of sales.
   b)   Any supply or service agreements.
   c)   A schedule of unfilled orders.
   d)   A description of the Company's major competitors.

9)   Litigation.
   a)   Copies of insurance policies possibly providing coverage as to pending or threatened litigation.
   b)   Documents relating to any injunctions, consent decrees, or settlements to which the Company is a party.
   c)   A list of unsatisfied judgments.

10)   Insurance Coverage.
   a)   A schedule and copies of the Company's general liability, personal and real property, product liability, errors and omissions, key-man, directors and officers, worker's compensation, and other insurance.